HANDBOOK OF FOREIGN AFFAIRS & DIPLOMACY OF SAARC COUNTRIES

Handbook of Foreign Affairs & Diplomacy of SAARC Countries

Puran Chandra

AKANSHA PUBLISHING HOUSE
NEW DELHI • GUWAHATI • VISAKHAPATNAM

AKANSHA PUBLISHING HOUSE
4649-B/21, Ansari Road
Darya Ganj, New Delhi - 110 002
Ph.: 23263193 / 9811582579 / 09435116718
Fax: 011-23263193
Email: ektabooks@yahoo.com
www.akanshapublishinghouse.com

Handbook of Foreign Affairs & Diplomacy of SAARC Countries

First Published 2010
ISBN 978-81-8370-217-1

PRINTED IN INDIA

Published by Akansha Publishing House, New Delhi and Printed at S.N. Printers, Delhi.

Contents

Preface

> "As the laws are above magistrates, so are the magistrates above the people; and it may truly be said, that the magistrate is a speaking law, and the law a silent magistrate."
>
> — *Cicero*

In fact, international relations, variously known as external affairs, foreign relations, foreign affairs and diplomacy is important branch of study. For smooth running of governance and existence of every nation-state international relations are of prime importance. Many theories and concepts are there which determine these relations of one country with another. These relations change according to contemporary happenings in the world order.

First, it is remarkable to note that a country's foreign policy, also called the international relations policy, is a set of goals outlining how the country will interact with other countries economically, politically, socially and militarily, and to a lesser extent, how the country will interact with non-state actors. The aforementioned interaction is evaluated and monitored in attempts to maximize benefits of multilateral international cooperation. Foreign policies are designed to help protect a country's national interests, national security, ideological goals, and economic prosperity. This can occur as a result of peaceful cooperation with other nations, or through exploitation. Usually, creating foreign policy is the job of the head of government and the foreign minister (or equivalent). In some countries the legislature also has considerable oversight. As an exception, in France and Finland, the head of state is responsible for foreign policy, while the head of government mainly deals with internal policy.

International relations (IR) represents the study of foreign affairs and global issues among states within the international system, including the roles of states, inter-governmental organizations (IGOs), non-governmental organizations (NGOs), international nongovernmental organizations (INGOs), and multinational corporations (MNCs). It is both an academic and public policy field, and can be either positive or normative as it both seeks to analyze as well as formulate the foreign policy of particular states. It is often considered a branch of political science (specially after 1988 UNESCO ncmenclature), but an important sector of academia prefer to treat it as an interdisciplinary field of study.

Besides political science, international relations draws upon such diverse fields as economics, history, international law, philosophy, geography, sociology, anthropology, psychology, and cultural studies. It involves a diverse range of issues including but not limited to: globalization, state sovereignty, ecological sustainability, nuclear proliferation, nationalism, economic development, global finance, terrorism, organized crime, human security, foreign interventionism and human rights.

In fact, history of international relations is often traced back to the Peace of Westphalia of 1648, where the modern state system was developed. Prior to this, the European medieval organization of political authority was based on a vaguely hierarchical religious order. Westphalia instituted the legal concept of sovereignty, which essentially meant that rulers, or the legitimate sovereigns, had no internal equals within a defined territory and no external superiors as the ultimate authority within the territory's sovereign borders.

As we know in present day context South Asia is the hotspot of crucial events having deep impact on world order and world peace. India and Pakistan are nuclear powers. India is emerging as a major leader in the world economy. The region is infested with the grave problem of terrorism. Pakistan is considered to harbour the terrorist outfits which have caused havoc. In Afghanistan US-led forces are fighting terrorism which have become on unending ongoing war. Taliban and other terrorist outfits like Al-Qaeda are still operative causing danger to world peace. India is badly suffering from the menace of terrorism in different parts of the country. Sri Lanka has undergone a long civil war against LTTE, which lasted recently on the ground. Bangladesh is aheading towards becoming a new harbour of terrorists. Political instability in Pakistan and Nepal are also major problems for the peace in the region. As such foreign relations of these countries are on dwindling pace.

The present work is devised as a handbook of diplomacy and foreign relations of SAARC countries. The following chapters make core of the study—Introduction; SAARC Countries: An Overview; Foreign Affairs of Afghanistan; Foreign Relations of Pakistan; Foreign Relations of Nepal; India's International Relations; Foreign Affairs of Bangladesh; Bhutan's External Affairs; Sri Lankan Foreign Relations; International Relations of Maldives; Appendix; Glossary and Bibliography etc.

Definitely, this will serve the purpose of students, teachers, researchers, policy planners and administrators besides the aspirants appearing for various competitive examinations.

For furnishing authoritative information, I have subscribed the views of different scholars in the field of diplomacy and international relations. As such sources of information are secondary i.e. published articles, books, magazines etc. available in print form of digitally, that two mainly websites. I am deeply beholden to all those scholars as well as the sources for benefiting from their works. My seniors, colleagues and friends have generously helped, inspired and guided me in my academic pursuits. I am grateful to them all.

I express my gratitude to my publishers for envincing keen interest in the present venture and materialising this in the present shape that too within shortest possible time.

I will be pleased if the learned readers could send their comments and suggestions for enhancing the quality of information contained herein.

— PC

1

Introduction

> "If you have ten men and only nine hats, the solution is not to cut off one head; it is, rather to make another hat."
>
> —*G.K. Chesterton*

In fact, international relations, variously known as external affairs, foreign relations, foreign affairs and diplomacy is important branch of study. For smooth running of governance and existence of every nation-state international relations are of prime importance. Many theories and concepts are there which determine these relations of one country with another. These relations change according to contemporary happenings in the world order.

A famous adage goes thus: "If you have the advantage over someone, and you , lead him to think that he has the advantage over you, without giving him the chance to take advantage of you- you are a diplomat." But diplomacy in the context of mutual coexistence and world peace must be based on certain humanitarian principles.

As the title of the book suggests, here we intend to furnish succinct information of foreign policy of SAARC countries. Before coming to main theme, we will highlight foreign policy and international relations with pros and cons. Then we will give an overview of SAARC countries which will be followed by salient features and latest developments in foreign policy of individual member countries of the SAARC.

First, it is remarkable to note that a country's foreign policy, also called the international relations policy, is a set of goals outlining how the country will interact with other countries economically, politically, socially and militarily, and to a lesser extent, how the country will interact with non-state actors. The aforementioned interaction is evaluated and monitored in attempts to maximize benefits of multilateral international cooperation. Foreign policies are designed to help protect a country's national interests, national security, ideological goals, and economic prosperity. This can occur as a result of peaceful cooperation with other nations, or through exploitation. Usually, creating foreign policy is the job of the head of government and the foreign minister (or equivalent). In some countries the legislature also has considerable oversight. As an exception, in France and Finland, the head of state is responsible for foreign policy, while the head of government mainly deals with internal policy. In the United States, the head of state (the President) also functions as the head of government.

International relations (IR) represents the study of foreign affairs and global issues among states within the international system, including the roles of states, inter-governmental organizations (IGOs), non-governmental organizations (NGOs), international nongovernmental organizations (INGOs), and multinational corporations (MNCs). It is both an academic and public policy field, and can be either positive or normative as it both seeks to analyze as well as formulate the foreign policy of particular states. It is often considered a branch of political science (specially after 1988 UNESCO nomenclature), but an important sector of academia prefer to treat it as an interdisciplinary field of study.

Besides political science, international relations draws upon such diverse fields as economics, history, international law, philosophy, geography, sociology, anthropology, psychology, and cultural studies. It involves a diverse range of issues including but not limited to: globalization, state sovereignty, ecological sustainability, nuclear proliferation, nationalism, economic development, global finance, terrorism, organized crime, human security, foreign interventionism and human rights.

In fact, history of international relations is often traced back to the Peace of Westphalia of 1648, where the modern state system was developed. Prior to this, the European medieval organization of political authority was based on a vaguely hierarchical religious order. Westphalia instituted the legal concept of sovereignty, which essentially meant that rulers, or the legitimate sovereigns, had no internal equals within a defined territory and no external superiors as the ultimate authority within the territory's sovereign borders.

A simple way to view this is that sovereignty says, "I'm not allowed to tell you what to do and you are not allowed to tell me what to do." Classical Greek and Roman authority at times resembled the Westphalian system, but both lacked the notion of sovereignty. Westphalia encouraged the rise of the independent nation-state, the institutionalization of diplomacy and armies. This particular European system was exported to the Americas, Africa, and Asia via colonialism and the "standards of civilization". The contemporary international system was finally established through decolonization during the Cold War. However, this is somewhat over-simplified. While the nation-state system is considered "modern", many states have not incorporated the system and are termed "pre-modern". Further, a handful of states have moved beyond the nation-state system and can be considered "post-modern". The ability of contemporary international relations discourse to explain the relations of these different types of states is disputed. "Levels of analysis" is a way of looking at the international system, which includes the individual level, the domestic nation-state as a unit, the international level of transnational and intergovernmental affairs, and the global level. What is explicitly recognized as International Relations theory was not developed until after World War I, and is dealt with in more detail below. IR theory, however, has a long tradition of drawing on the work of other social sciences. The use of capitalizations of the "I" and "R" in International Relations aims to distinguish the academic discipline of International Relations from the phenomena of international relations.

Similarly, liberalism draws upon the work of Kant and Rousseau, with the work of the former often being cited as the first elaboration of democratic peace theory. Though contemporary human rights is considerably different than the type of rights envisioned under natural law, Francisco de Vitoria, Hugo Grotius and John Locke offered the first accounts of universal entitlement to certain rights on the basis of common humanity. In the twentieth century, in addition to contemporary theories of liberal internationalism, Marxism has been a foundation of international relations.

In fact, international relations as a distinct field of study was almost entirely British-centered. In 1919, the Chair in International Politics established at the University of Wales, Aberystwyth (renamed Aberystwyth University in 2008), from an endowment given by David Davies, became the first academic position dedicated to international relations. In the early 1920s, the London School of Economics' department of International Relations was founded at the behest of Nobel Peace Prize winner Philip Noel-Baker. The first university entirely dedicated to the study of international relations was the Graduate Institute of International Studies (now the Graduate Institute of International and Development Studies), which was founded in 1927 to form diplomats associated to the League of Nations, established in Geneva some years before. The Graduate Institute of International Studies offered one of the first Ph.D. degrees in international relations. Georgetown University's Edmund A. Walsh School of Foreign Service is the oldest international relations faculty in the United States, founded in 1919. The Committee on International Relations at the University of Chicago was the first to offer a graduate degree, in 1928.

Major Theories

Epistemology and International Relations Theory

International relations theories can be roughly divided into one of two epistemological camps: "positivist" and "post-positivist". Positivist theories aim to replicate the methods of the natural sciences by analysing the impact of material forces. They typically focus on features of international relations such as state interactions, size of military forces, balance of powers etc. Post-positivist epistemology rejects the idea that the social world can be studied in an objective and value-free way. It rejects the central ideas of neo-realism/liberalism, such as rational choice theory, on the grounds that the scientific method cannot be applied to the social world and that a 'science' of international relations is impossible. A key difference between the two positions is that while positivist theories, such as neo-realism, offer causal explanations (such as why and how power is exercised), post-positivist theories focus instead on constitutive questions, for instance what is meant by 'power'; what makes it up, how it is experienced and how it is reproduced. Often, post-positivist theories explicitly promote a normative approach to international relations, by considering ethics.

This is something which has often been ignored under 'traditional' international relations as positivist theories make a distinction between 'facts' and normative judgments, or 'values'. During the late 1980s/1990 debate between positivists and post-positivists became the dominant debate and has been described as constituting the Third "Great Debate" (Lapid 1989).

Positivist Theories

1. Liberal Internationalism: Liberal international relations theory arose after World War I in response to the inability of states to control and limit war in their international relations. Early adherents include Woodrow Wilson and Norman Angell, who argued vigorously that states mutually gained from cooperation and that war was so destructive to be essentially futile. Liberalism was not recognized as a coherent theory as such until it was collectively and derisively termed idealism by E. H. Carr. A new version of "idealism" that focused on human rights as the basis of the legitimacy of international law was advanced by Hans Köchler.

2. Realism: Realism focuses on state security and power above all else. Early realists such as E.H. Carr and Hans Morgenthau argued that states are self-interested, power-seeking rational actors, who seek to maximize theinternational relationssecurity and chances of survival. Any cooperation between states is explained as functional in order to maximize each individual state's security (as opposed to more idealistic reasons). Many realists saw World War II as the vindication of their theory. It should be noted that classical writers such as Thucydides, Machiavelli, and Hobbes are often cited as "founding fathers" of realism by contemporary self-described realists. However, while their work may support realist doctrine, it is not likely that they would have classified themselves as realists (in this sense of the term). Realists are often split up into two groups: Classical or Human Nature Realists (as described here) and Structural or Neorealists (below).

3. *Regime Theory:* Regime theory is derived from the liberal tradition that argues that international institutions or regimes affect the behavior of states (or other international actors). It assumes that cooperation is possible in the anarchic system of states, indeed, regimes are by definition, instances of international cooperation. While realism predicts that conflict should be the norm in international relations, regime theorists say that there is cooperation despite anarchy. Often they cite cooperation in trade, human rights and collective security among other issues. These instances of cooperation are regimes. The most commonly cited definition of regimes comes from Stephen Krasner. Krasner defines regimes as "institutions possessing norms, decision rules, and procedures which facilitate a convergence of expectations." Not all approaches to regime theory, however are liberal or neoliberal; some realist scholars like Joseph Greico have developed hybrid theories which take a realist based approach to this fundamentally liberal theory

4. *Neoliberalism:* Neoliberalism seeks to update liberalism by accepting the neorealist presumption that states are the key actors in international relations, but still maintains that non-state actors (NSAs) and intergovernmental organizations (IGOs) matter. Proponents such as Maria

Chattha argue that states will cooperate irrespective of relative gains, and are thus concerned with absolute gains.

This also means that nations are, in essence, free to make their own choices as to how they will go about conducting policy without any international organizations blocking a nation's right to sovereignty. Neoliberalism also contains an economic theory that is based on the use of open and free markets with little, if any, government intervention to prevent monopolies and other conglomerates from forming. The growing interdependence throughout and after the Cold War through international institutions led to neo-liberalism being defined as institutionalism, this new part of the theory being fronted by Robert Keohane and also Joseph Nye.

Post-Positivist/reflectivist Theories

1. International society theory: International society theory, also called the English School, focuses on the shared norms and values of states and how they regulate international relations. Examples of such norms include diplomacy, order, and international law. Unlike neo-realism, it is not necessarily positivist. Theorists have focused particularly on humanitarian intervention, and are subdivided between solidarists, who tend to advocate it more, and pluralists, who place greater value in order and sovereignty. Nicholas Wheeler is a prominent solidarist, while Hedley Bull and Robert H. Jackson are perhaps the best known pluralists.

2. Social Constructivism: Social Constructivism encompasses a broad range of theories that aim to address questions of ontology, such as the Structure and agency debate, as well as questions of epistemology, such as the "material/ideational" debate that concerns the relative role of material forces versus ideas. Constructivism is not a theory of international relations in the manner of neo-realism, but is instead a social theory which is used to better explain the actions taken by states and other major actors as well as the identities that guide these states and actors. Constructivism in international relations can be divided into what Hopf (1998) calls 'conventional' and 'critical' constructivism. Common to all varieties of constructivism is an interest in the role that ideational forces play. The most famous constructivist scholar, Alexander Wendt noted in a 1992 article in International Organization that "anarchy is what states make of it". By this he means that the anarchical structure that neo-realists claim governs state interaction is in fact a phenomenon that is socially constructed and reproduced by states. For example, if the system is dominated by states that see anarchy as a life or death situation (what Wendt terms a "Hobbesian" anarchy) then the system will be characterised by warfare. If on the other hand anarchy is seen as restricted (a "Lockean" anarchy) then a more peaceful system will exist.

3. *Marxism:* Marxist and Neo-Marxist theories of international relations reject the realist/liberal view of state conflict or cooperation; instead focusing on the economic and material aspects. It makes the assumption that the economy trumps other concerns; allowing for the elevation of class as the focus of study. Marxists view the international system as an integrated capitalist system in pursuit of capital accumulation. Thus, the period of colonialism brought in sources for raw materials and captive markets for exports, while decolonialization brought new opportunities in the form of dependence. Linked in with Marxist theories is dependency theory which argues that developed countries, in their pursuit of power, penetrate developing states through political advisors, missionaries, experts and MNCs to integrate

them into the integrated capitalist system in order to appropriate natural resources and foster dependence by developing countries on developed countries. Marxist theories receive scant attention in the United States where no significant socialist party ever existed. It is more common in parts of Europe and is one of the most important theoretic contributions of Latin American academia, for example through Liberation theology.

4. Critical Theory: Critical international relations theory is the application of 'critical theory' to international relations. Proponents such as Andrew Linklater, Robert W. Cox and Ken Booth focus on the need for human emancipation from States. Hence, it is "critical" of mainstream internatinal relations international relations theories that tend to be state-centric.

Leadership Theories

1. Interest Group theory posits that the driving force behind state behavior is sub-state interest groups. Examples interest groups include political lobbyists, the military, and the corporate sector. Group theory argues that although these interest groups are constitutive of the state, they are also causal forces in the exercise of state power.

2. Strategic Perspective is a theoretical approach that views individuals as choosing their actions by taking into account the anticipated actions and responses of others with the intention of maximizing their own welfare.

Major Concepts

1. Systemic Level Concepts: International relations is often viewed in terms of levels of analysis, the systemic level concepts are those broad concepts that define and shape an international milieu, characterised by Anarchy.

2. *Conjuncture:* In decision making in international relations, the concept of International Conjuncture, together with freedom of action and equality are important elements. Decision makers must take into account the set of international conditions in taking initiatives that would create different types of responses.

Power: The concept of power in international relations can be described as the degree of resources, capabilities, and influence in international affairs. It is often divided up into the concepts of hard power and soft power, hard power relating primarily to coercive power, such as the use of force, and soft power commonly covering economics, diplomacy and cultural influence. However, there is no clear dividing line between the two forms of power.

Polarity: Polarity in International Relations refers to the arrangement of power within the international system. The concept arose from bipolarity during the Cold War, with the international system dominated by the conflict between two superpowers, and has been applied retrospectively. Consequently, the international system prior to 1945 can be described as multi-polar, with power being shared among Great powers.

Remarkably, the collapse of the Soviet Union in 1991 had led to what some would call unipolarity, with the United States as a sole superpower. However, due to China's surge of economic success after joining the World Trade Organization in 2001, combined with the respectable international position they hold within political spheres and the power that the Chinese Government exerts over their people (consisting of the largest population in the world), there is debate over whether China is now a superpower or a possible candidate in the future. Several theories of international relations draw upon the idea of polarity. The balance of power was a concept prevalent in Europe prior to the World War II the thought being that by balancing power blocs it would create stability and prevent war. Theories of the balance of power gained prominence again during the Cold War, being a central mechanism of Kenneth Waltz's Neorealism. Here, the concepts of balancing (rising in power to counter another) and bandwagonning (siding with another) are developed.

Further, Hegemonic stability theory (developed by Robert Gilpin) also draws upon the idea of Polarity, specifically the state of unipolarity. Hegemony is the preponderance of power at one pole in the international system, and the theory argues this is a stable configuration because of mutual gains by both the dominant power and others in the international system. This is contrary to many Neorealist arguments, particularly made by Kenneth Waltz, stating that the end of the Cold War and the state of unipolarity is an unstable configuration that will inevitably change.

This can be expressed in Power transition theory, which states that it is likely that a great power would challenge a hegemon after a certain period, resulting in a major war. It suggests that while hegemony can control the occurrence of wars, it also results in the creation of one.

Interdependence: Many advocate that the current international system is characterized by growing interdependence; the mutual responsibility and dependency on others. Advocates of this point to growing globalization, particularly with international economic interaction. The role of international institutions, and widespread acceptance of a number of operating principles in the international system, reinforces ideas that relations are characterized by interdependence.

Further Dependency theory is a theory most commonly associated with Marxism, stating that a set of Core states exploit a set of weaker Periphery states for their prosperity. Various versions of the theory suggest that this is either an inevitability (standard dependency theory), or use the theory to highlight the necessity for change (Neo-Marxist).

Tools and Strategies

1. Sanctions are usually a first resort after the failure of diplomacy, and are one of the main tools used to enforce treaties. They can take the form of diplomatic or economic sanctions and involve the cutting of ties and imposition of barriers to communication or trade.

2. Diplomacy is the practice of communication and negotiation between representatives of states. To some extent, all other tools of international relations can be considered the failure of diplomacy. Keeping in mind, the use of other tools are part of the communication and negotiation inherent within diplomacy. Sanctions, force, and adjusting trade regulations, while not typically considered part of diplomacy, are actually valuable tools in the interest of leverage and placement in negotiations.

3. War, the use of force, is often thought of as the ultimate tool of international relations. A widely accepted definition is that given by Clausewitz, with war being "the continuation of politics by other means". There is a growing study into 'new wars' involving actors other than states. The study of war in International Relations is covered by the disciplines of 'War Studies' and 'Strategic studies'.

4. The mobilization of international shame can also be thought of as a tool of International Relations. This is attempting to alter states' actions through 'naming and shaming' at the international level. This is mostly done by

the large human rights NGOs such as Amnesty International (for instance when it called Guantanamo Bay a "Gulag"), or Human Rights Watch. A prominent use of was the UN Commission on Human Rights 1235 procedure, which publicly exposes state's human rights violations. The current Human Rights Council has yet to use this mechanism.

5. The allotment of economic and/or diplomatic benefits. An example of this is the European Union's enlargement policy. Candidate countries are allowed entry into the EU only after the fulfillment of the Copenhagen criteria.

As a level of analysis the unit level is often referred to as the state level, as it locates its explanation at the level of the state, rather than the international system.

Regime type: It is often considered that a state's form of government can dictate the way that a state interacts with others in the international system.

Democratic Peace Theory is a theory that suggests that the nature of democracy means that democratic countries will not go to war with each other. The justifications for this are that democracies externalise their norms and only go to war for just causes, and that democracy encourages mutual trust and respect.

Communism justifies a world revolution, which similarly would lead to peaceful coexistence, based on a proletarian global society.

Revisionism/Status quo Theory

States can be classified by whether they accept the international status quo, or are revisionist, i.e. want change. Revisionist states seek to fundamentally change the rules and practices of international relations, feeling disadvantaged by the status quo. They see the international system as a largely western creation which serves to reinforce current realities. Japan is an example of a state that has gone from being a revisionist state to one that is satisfied with the status quo, because the status quo is now beneficial to it.

Religion: It is often considered that religion can have an effect on the way a state acts within the international system. Religion is visible as an organising principle particularly for Islamic states, whereas secularism sits at the other end of the spectrum, with the separation of state and religion being responsible for the Liberal international relations theory.

The level beneath the unit (state) level can be useful both for explaining factors in International Relations that other theories fail to explain, and for moving away from a state-centric view of international relations.

1. *Bureaucratic politics* - Looks at the role of the bureaucracy in decision making, and sees decisions as a result of bureaucratic in-fighting, and as having been shaped by various constraints.
2. *Psychological factors in International Relations* - Evaluating psychological factors in international relations comes from the understanding that a state is not a 'black box' as proposed by Realism, and that there may be other influences on foreign policy decisions. Examining the role of personalities in the decision making process can have some explanatory power, as can the role of misperception between various actors. A prominent application of sub-unit level psychological factors in international relations is the concept of Groupthink, another is the propensity of policymakers to think in terms of analogies.

3. Religious, Ethnic, and secessionist groups - Viewing these aspects of the sub-unit level has explanatory power with regards to ethnic conflicts, religious wars, transnational diaspora (diaspora politics) and other actors which do not consider themselves to fit with the defined state boundaries. This is particularly useful in the context of the pre-modern world of weak states.
4. Science, Technology and International Relations- How science and technology impact the global health, business, environment, technology, and development.
5. International political economy, and economic factors in international relations.

International institutions form a vital part of contemporary International Relations. Much interaction at the system level is governed by them, and they outlaw some traditional institutions and practices of International Relations, such as the use of war (except in self-defence). As humanity enters the Planetary phase of civilization, some scientists and political theorists see a global hierarchy of institutions replacing the existing system of sovereign nation-states as the primary political community. They argue that nations are an imagined community that cannot resolve such modern challenges as the "Dogville" effect (strangers in a homogeneous community), the legal and political status of stateless people and refugees, and the need to address worldwide concerns like climate change and pandemics. Futurist Paul Raskin has hypothesized that a new, more legitimate form of global politics could be based on "constrained pluralism." This principle guides the formation of institutions based on three characteristics: irreducibility, where some issues must be adjudicated at the global level; subsidiarity, which limits the scope of global authority to truly global issues while smaller-scope issues are regulated at lower levels; and heterogeneity, which allows for diverse forms of local and regional institutions as long as they meet global obligations.

Role of United Nations

The United Nations (UN) is an international organization that describes itself as a "global association of governments facilitating co-operation in international law, international security, economic development, and social equity"; It is the most prominent international institution. Many of the legal institutions follow the same organizational structure as the UN.

Economic Institutions

- Asian Development Bank
- African Development Bank
- Inter-American Development Bank
- International Monetary Fund
- World Bank
- World Trade Organization

International Legal Bodies

Human Rights

- European Court of Human Rights
- Human Rights Committee
- Inter-American Court of Human Rights
- International Criminal Court
- International Criminal Tribunal for Rwanda
- International Criminal Tribunal for the Former Yugoslavia
- United Nations Human Rights Council

Legal

- African Court of Justice
- European Court of Justice
- International Court of Justice
- International Tribunal for the Law of the Sea

We have given an elaborate description of foreign relation with academic analysis in the next chapter we will give an overview of SAARC counties. The subsequent chaptrs with highlight the basic facts of international relations and diplomacy of individual members countries of the SAARC.

REFERENCES

1. Barry Buzan *Regions and Powers,* 2003.
2. Daniel Deudney *Bounding Power: The Republican Security Theory from the Polis to the Global Village.*
3. Hugo Grotius, *The Laws of War and Peace.*
4. Robert H. Jackson *The Global Covenant* 2002.
5. Hans Köchler, *Aussenpolitik und Demokratie* (German), 1986 (Foreign Policy and Democracy).
6. Donald Markwell, *John Maynard Keynes and International Relations: Economic Paths to War and Peace*, 2006.

2

SAARC Countries: An Overview

SAARC (South Asian Association for Regional Cooperation) emerged a bloc with the aim of mutual cooperatio9n for prosperity and well being of member countries in south Asia.

BASIC FACTS	
Headquarters	Kathmandu, Nepal
Membership	8 member states 6 observers
— Chairman	Mahinda Rajapaksa
— Secretary General	Sheel Kant Sharma
Establishment	December 8, 1985
— Total Area	5,130,746 km (7th) (1,980,992 sq mi)
Population	1,467,255,669 (1st) 2004 estimate
— Density	285.9/km (740.5/sq mi)
GDP (PPP)	2005 estimate
— Total	US$ 4,074,031 million (3rd[1])
— Per capita	US$ 2,777
Time zone	(UTC+4½ to +6)

Source: Websitehttp://www.saarc-sec.org/

Basically, South Asian Association for Regional Cooperation (SAARC) is an economic and political organization of eight countries in Southern Asia. In terms of population, its sphere of influence is the largest of any regional organization: almost 1.5 billion people, the combined population of its member states. It was established on December 8, 1985 by Bangladesh, Bhutan, Maldives, Nepal, Pakistan, India and Sri Lanka. In April 2007, at the Association's 14th summit, Afghanistan became its eighth member.

Now we will come to history of the emergence of SAARC in the late 1970s, Bangladeshi President Ziaur Rahman proposed the creation of a trade bloc consisting of South Asian countries. The idea of regional cooperation in South Asia was again mooted in May 1980. The foreign secretaries of the seven countries met for the first time in Colombo in April 1981. The Committee of the Whole, which met in Colombo in August 1981, identified five broad areas for regional cooperation. New areas of cooperation were added in the following years.

The objectives of the Association as defined in the Charter are:

(a) to promote the welfare of the people of South Asia and to improve their quality of life;

(b) to accelerate economic growth, social progress and cultural development in the region and to provide all individuals the opportunity to live in dignity and to realize their full potential;

(c) to promote and strengthen collective self-reliance among the countries of South Asia;

(d) to contribute to mutual trust, understanding and appreciation of one another's problems;

(e) to promote active collaboration and mutual assistance in the economic, social, cultural, technical and scientific fields;

(f) to strengthen cooperation with other developing countries;

(g) to strengthen cooperation among themselves in international forums on matters of common interest; and

(h) to cooperate with international and regional organisations with similar aims and purposes.

The Declaration on South Asian Regional Cooperation was adopted by the Foreign Ministers in 1983 in New Delhi. During the meeting, the Ministers also launched the Integrated Programme of Action (IPA) in nine agreed areas, namely, Agriculture; Rural Development; Telecommunications; Meteorology; Health and Population Activities; Transport; Postal Services; Science and Technology; and Sports, Arts and Culture. The South Asian Association for Regional Cooperation (SAARC) was established when its Charter was formally adopted on 8 December 1985 by the Heads of State or Government of Bangladesh, Bhutan, India, Maldives, Nepal, Pakistan and Sri Lanka.

Afghanistan was added to the regional grouping at the behest of India on 13 November 2005, and became a member on 3 April 2007. With the addition of Afghanistan, the total number of member states were raised to eight. In April 2006, the United States of America and South Korea made formal requests to be granted observer status. The European Union has also indicated interest in being given observer status, and made a formal request for the same to the SAARC Council of Ministers meeting in July 2006. On 2 August 2006 the foreign ministers of the SAARC countries agreed in principle to grant observer status to the US, South Korea and the European Union. On 4 March 2007,

Iran requested observer status. Followed shortly by of Mauritius as new entrant.

Secretariat

The SAARC Secretariat was established in Kathmandu on 16 January 1987 and was inaugurated by Late King Birendra Bir Bikram Shah of Nepal. It is headed by a Secretary General appointed by the Council of Ministers from Member Countries in alphabetical order for a three-year term. He is assisted by the Professional and the General Services Staff, and also an appropriate number of functional units called Divisions assigned to Directors on deputation from Member States.

The Secretariat coordinates and monitors implementation of activities, prepares for and services meetings, and serves as a channel of communication between the Association and its Member States as well as other regional organizations. The Memorandum of Understanding on the establishment of the Secretariat which was signed by Foreign Ministers of member countries on 17 November 1986 at Bangalore, India contains various clauses concerning the role, structure and administration of the SAARC Secretariat as well as the powers of the Secretary-General.

In several recent meetings the heads of state or government of member states of SAARC have taken some important decisions and bold initiatives to strengthen the organisation and to widen and deepen regional co-operation. The SAARC Secretariat and Member States observe 8 December as the SAARC Charter Day.

But SAARC could not play the strong role. SAARC 's inability to play a crucial role in integrating South Asia is often credited to the political and military rivalry between India and Pakistan. Over the years, SAARC's role in South

Asia has been greatly diminished and is now used as a mere platform for annual talks and meetings between its members.

In fact, SAARC has intentionally laid more stress on "core issues" mentioned above rather than more decisive political issues like the Kashmir dispute and the Sri Lankan civil war. However, political dialogue is often conducted on the margins of SAARC meetings. SAARC has also refrained itself from interfering in the internal matters of its member states. During the 12th and 13th SAARC summits, extreme emphasis was laid upon greater cooperation between the SAARC members to fight terrorism.

Over the years, the SAARC members have expressed their unwillingness on signing a free trade agreement. Though India has several trade pacts with Maldives, Nepal, Bhutan and Sri Lanka, similar trade agreements with Pakistan and Bangladesh have been stalled due to political and economic concerns on both sides. India has been constructing a barrier across its borders with Bangladesh and Pakistan. In 1993, SAARC countries signed an agreement to gradually lower tariffs within the region, in Dhaka. Eleven years later, at the 12th SAARC Summit at Islamabad, SAARC countries devised the South Asia Free Trade Agreement which created a framework for the establishment of a free trade area covering 1.4 billion people. This agreement went into force on January 1, 2006. Under this agreement, SAARC members will bring their duties down to 20 per cent by 2007.

It is worth mentining the Dhaka 2005 summit accorded observer status to People's Republic of China, Japan, South Korea and United States of America. The nations also agreed to organize development funds under a single financial institution with a permanent secretariat, that would cover all SAARC programs and also ranging from social, to infrastructure, to economic ones.

Current Members

1. Afghanistan
2. Bangladesh
3. Bhutan
4. India
5. Maldives
6. Nepal
7. Pakistan
8. Sri Lanka

Observers

1. Australia
2. China
3. European Union
4. Iran
5. Japan
6. Mauritius
7. Myanmar (Burma)
8. South Korea
9. United States of America.

Latest Development

The People's Republic of China has shown its interest in joining SAARC. While Pakistan and Bangladesh support China's candidature, India is more reluctant about the prospect of Chinese membership, while Bhutan does not even have diplomatic relations with China. However, during the 2005 Dhaka summit, India agreed on granting observer status to the PRC along with Japan. During the 14th summit, Nepal along with Pakistan and Bangladesh, announced their support for the membership of China. China seeks greater involvement in SAARC, however, finds it too early to apply for full membership. Indonesia intends to become an observer as well, and is supported by Sri Lanka.

Iran, a state with borders to two SAARC members, has traditionally enjoyed strong cultural, economic and political relationships with Afghanistan, Pakistan, India and Bangladesh and has expressed its desire to become a member of the South Asian organization. On 22 February 2005, the Foreign Minister of Iran, Kamal Kharrazi, indicated Iran's interest in joining SAARC by saying that his country could provide the region with "East-West connectivity". On 3 March 2007, Iran asked to join the SAARC as an observer. SAARC Secretary-General Lyonpo Chenkyab Dorji responded by saying that Iran's request for observer status would be taken up during a meeting of ministers of foreign affairs of SAARC member countries in the 3 April summit in New Delhi.

Russia intends to become an observer as well, and is supported by India. Myanmar has expressed an interest in joining as a full member. If done so, Myanmar will become the ninth member in the group. India is currently backing Myanmar. Burma's military regime officially applied for full SAARC membership in May 2008. However, the application is still being considered and the government is currently restricted to observer status. South Africa has participated in meetings.

Secretaries General

Abul Ahsan	January 16, 1987 to 15 October 1989
Kant Kishore Bhargava	October 17, 1989 to December 31, 1991
Ibrahim Hussain Zaki	January 1, 1992 to December 31, 1993
Yadav Kant Silwal	January 1, 1994 to December 31, 1995
Naeem U. Hasan	January 1, 1996 to December 31, 1998
Nihal Rodrigo	January 1, 1999 to January 10, 2002
Q.A.M.A. Rahim	January 11, 2002 to February 28, 2005
Lyonpo Chenkyab Dorji	March 1, 2005 to February 29, 2008
Sheel Kant Sharma	March 1, 2008 to present

SAARC Summits

1st	Dhaka	December 7-8 1985
2nd	Bangalore	November 16-17 1986
3rd	Kathmandu	November 2-4 1987
4th	Islamabad	December 29-31 1988
5th	Malé	November 21-23 1990
6th	Colombo	December 21, 1991
7th	Dhaka	April 10-11 1993
8th	New Delhi	May 2-4 1995
9th	Malé	May 12-14 1997
10th	Colombo	July 29-31 1998
11th	Kathmandu	January 4-6 2002
12th	Islamabad	January 2-6 2004
13th	Dhaka	November 12-13 2005
14th	New Delhi	April 3-4 2007
15th	Colombo	August 1-3 2008
16th	Male	
17th	Bhutan	Scheduled to held in 2010

SAPTA

The Agreement on SAARC Preferential Trading Arrangement (SAPTA) was signed on 11 April 1993 and entered into force on 7 December 1995, with the desire of the Member States of SAARC (India, Pakistan, Nepal, Sri Lanka, Bangladesh, Bhutan and the Maldives) to promote and sustain mutual trade and economic cooperation within the SAARC region through the exchange of concessions.The establishment of an Inter-Governmental Group (IGG) to formulate an agreement to establish a SAPTA by 1997 was approved in the *Sixth Summit of SAARC* held in Colombo in December 1991.

The basic principles underlying SAPTA are:

1. *overall reciprocity* and *mutuality of advantages* so as to benefit equitably all Contracting States, taking into account their respective level of economic and industrial development, the pattern of their external trade, and trade and tariff policies and systems;
2. negotiation of *tariff reform* step by step, improved and extended in successive stages through periodic reviews;
3. recognition of the special needs of the Least Developed Contracting States and agreement on *concrete preferential measures* in their favour;
4. inclusion of all products, manufactures and commodities in their raw, semi-processed and processed forms.

So far, four rounds of trade negotiations have been concluded under SAPTA covering over 5000 commodities.

South Asian Free Trade Area

The Agreement on the South Asian Free Trade Area is an agreement reached at the 12th SAARC summit at Islamabad, capital of Pakistan on 6 January 2004. It creates a framework for the creation of a free trade area covering 1.4 billion people in India, Pakistan, Nepal, Sri Lanka,

Bangladesh, Bhutan and the Maldives.The seven foreign ministers of the region signed a framework agreement on SAFTA with zero customs duty on the trade of practically all products in the region by end 2016. The new agreement i.e. SAFTA, came into being on 1 January 2006 and will be operational following the ratification of the agreement by the seven governments. SAFTA requires the developing countries in South Asia, that is, India, Pakistan and Sri Lanka, to bring their duties down to 20 percent in the first phase of the two year period ending in 2007. In the final five year phase ending 2012, the 20 percent duty will be reduced to zero in a series of annual cuts. The least developed nations in South Asia consisting of Nepal, Bhutan, Bangladesh and Maldives have an additional three years to reduce tariffs to zero. Pakistan has signed but not ratified the treaty, though there is hope in India, that it will sometime in 2008.

As we know in present day context south Asia is the hot spot of crucial events. India and Pakistan are nuclear power. India is emerging as a major leader in the world economy. The region is infested with the grave problem of terrorism. Pakistan is considered to harbour the terrorist outfits which have caused havoc. In Afghanistan US-led forces are fighting terrorism which have become on unending ongoing war. Taliban and other terrorist outfits like Al-Qaeda are still operative causing danger to world peace. India is badly suffering from the menace of terrorism in different parts of the country. Sri Lanka has undergone a long civil war against LTTE, which lasted recently on the ground. Bangladesh is aheading towards becoming a new harbour of terrorists. Political instability in Pakistan and Nepal are also major problems for the peace in the region. As such foreign relations of these countries are on dwindling pace.

Hereafter we will portray the actual picture of foreign policy of individual member countries of the SAARC separately.

REFERENCES

A Brief on SAARC." South Asian Association for Regional Cooperation. No date.

"Afghanistan to be new SAARC member." *Times of India*, 13 November 2005.

Breffni O'Rourke. "South Asia: Afghanistan Joins World's Largest Regional Grouping." Radio Free Europe/Radio Liberty, 3 April 2007.

Charter of the South Asian Association for Regional Cooperation, Article 1.

"SAARC to grant observer status to US, S Korea, EU." *Hindustan Times.* 2 August 2006.

Waliur Rahman. "US and S Korea to observe SAARC." BBC News, 11 April 2006.

3

Foreign Affairs of Afghanistan

Afghanistan or the Islamic Republic of Afghanistan, is a landlocked country that is located approximately in the center of Asia. It is variously designated as geographically located within Central Asia, South Asia, and the Middle East. It is bordered by Pakistan in the south and east, Iran in the south and west, Turkmenistan, Uzbekistan and Tajikistan in the north, and China in the far northeast. Afghanistan is a crossroads between the East and the West, and has been an ancient focal point of trade and migration. It has an important geostrategical location, connecting South and Central Asia and Middle East.

BASIC FACTS

Capital	Kabul
Official languages	Dari (Persian), Pashto
Government	Islamic republic
• President	Hamid Karzai
Establishment	
• First Afghan state	October 1747
• Independence from UK	August 19, 1919
Area	
• Total	647,500 km (251,772 sq mi)
• Water (%)	0

Population	
• 2008 estimate	32,738,376
• 1979 census	13,051,358
• Density	46/km (119/sq mi)
GDP (PPP)	2008 estimate
• Total	$21.340 billion
• Per capita	$758
GDP (nominal)	2008 estimate
• Total	$12.061 billion
• Per capita	$428
HDI (1993)	0.229 (n/a) (unranked)
Currency	Afghani (AFN)

It is remarkable that foreign relations of Afghanistan, like those of any country, have changed along with the political, sociological, and economic state of the various parts of Afghanistan.

Notably, before the Soviet invasion, Afghanistan pursued a policy of neutrality and nonalignment in its foreign relations, being one of a few independent nations to stay neutral in both World War I and World War II. In international forums, Afghanistan generally followed the voting patterns of Asian and African non-aligned countries. During the 1950s and 60s, Afghanistan was able to use the Russian and American need for allies during the Cold War as a way to receive economic assistance from both countries. However, given that unlike Russia, America refused to give extensive military aid to the country, the government of Mohammed Daoud Khan developed warmer ties with the USSR while officially remaining non-aligned.

Following the Marxist coup of April 1978, the Taraki government developed significantly closer ties with the

Soviet Union and its communist satellites. After the December 1979 invasion, Afghanistan's foreign policy mirrored that of the Soviet Union. Afghan foreign policymakers attempted, with little success, to increase their regime's low standing in the noncommunist world. With the signing of the Geneva Accords, President Najibullah unsuccessfully sought to end the Democratic Republic of Afghanistan's isolation within the Islamic world and in the Non-Aligned Movement. Most Western countries, including the United States, maintained small diplomatic missions in the capital city of Kabul during the Soviet occupation. Many countries subsequently closed their missions due to instability and heavy fighting in Kabul after the Soviet withdrawal in 1989.

Notably, Afghanistan participated in the 1991 Gulf War against Iraq. Many countries initially welcomed the introduction of the Taliban, who they saw as a stabilizing, law-enforcing alternative to the warlords who had ruled the country since the fall of Najibullah's government in 1992. The Taliban soon became alienated of those countries' positive feelings with knowledge of the harsh Sharia law being enforced in Taliban-controlled territories spreading around the world.

The brutality towards women who attempted to work, learn, or leave the house without a male escort caused outside aid to the war-torn country to be limited. Repeated Taliban efforts to occupy Afghanistan's seat at the UN and OIC were unsuccessful. By 2001, only Pakistan, Saudi Arabia, and the United Arab Emirates recognized the Taliban as the legitimate government of Afghanistan.

All three countries withdrew recognition to the Taliban in the months following the September 11, 2001 terrorist attack on the United States. Following the American Invasion and the Bonn Agreement the new government under the leadership of Hamid Karzai started to re-establish diplomatic relationships with many countries who had held close diplomatic relations before the communist coup d'état and the subsequent civil war.

Remarkably, the government of President Hamid Karzai is currently focused on securing continued assistance for rebuilding the economy, infrastructure, and military of the country. It has continued to maintain close ties with the United States, India, Iran, the European Union, and the Islamic world. Now we will give Afghanistan foreign relation with different countries.

With Pakistan

Notably, two areas—NWFP and Balochistan—have long complicated Afghanistan's relations with Pakistan. Controversies involving these areas date back to the establishment of the Durand Line in 1893 dividing Pashtun and Baluch tribes living in Afghanistan from those living in what later became Pakistan. Afghanistan vigorously protested the inclusion of Pashtun and Baluch areas within Pakistan without providing the inhabitants with an opportunity for self-determination. Since 1947, this problem has led to incidents along the border, with extensive disruption of normal trade patterns.

The most serious crisis lasted from September 1961 to June 1963, when diplomatic, trade, transit, and consular relations between the countries were suspended. The 1978 Marxist coup further strained relations between the two countries. Pakistan took the lead diplomatically in the United Nations, the Non-Aligned Movement, and the Organization of the Islamic Conference in opposing the Soviet occupation. During the war against the Soviet occupation, Pakistan served as the primary logistical conduit for the Afghan resistance.

Pakistan, aided by UN agencies, private groups, and many friendly countries, continues to provide refuge to several million Afghans. Pakistan developed close ties to the Taliban regime, which it believed would offer strategic depth in any future conflict with India, and extended recognition in 1997. Following the 2001 invasion and overthrow of the Taliban, Pakistan recognized the transitional administration led by Hamid Karzai and offered significant amounts of aid and continued relief to Afghan refugees living in Pakistan. As of 2006, Afghan-Pakistani relations continue to fluctuate due to continued controversy over the Durand Line and Afghanistan's close relationship with India. Much of Afghanistan has long relied on Pakistani links for trade and travel to the outside world, and Pakistan views Afghanistan as eventually becoming its primary route for trade with Central Asia, though these plans will of necessity await establishment of secure conditions. On the other hand, Pakistan has a two faced policy for Afghanistan. That is because of Durand Line Opposition between these two countries, the situation is becoming worse day by day. Many many Afghans believe that Pakistan is an agent of Western countries, strengthening the diplomatic attempts of them.

Others however are more pragmatic and seek to form a confederation with Pakistan. Such a confederation would in essence, re-establish the original Afghanistan minus Nishapur in Iran as created by the founder Ahmed Shah Abdali. Prominent European and North American scholars believe that such a union would bring peace and stability to both countries and in lieu of history would be the natural route to go for the better interest of both these countries, their peoples and the region as a whole.

With Iran

Remarkably, Afghanistan shares a long history with Iran, as the nation was once a part of ancient Persia. There are also deep ties in language and culture, as an eastern dialect of Persian (Dari Persian) is the dominant language of Afghanistan, especially in terms of education and business. Despite such close ties, Afghanistan's relations with Iran have fluctuated over the years, with periodic disputes over the water rights of the Helmand River as the main issue of contention. Following the Soviet invasion of Afghanistan, which Iran opposed, relations deteriorated. The Iranian consulate in Herat closed, as did the Afghan consulate in Mashad. The Iranians complained of periodic border violations following the Soviet invasion. In 1985, they urged feuding Afghan Shi'a resistance groups to unite to oppose the Soviets. Iran supported the cause of the Afghan resistance and provided limited financial and military assistance to rebel leaders who pledged loyalty to the Iranian vision of Islamic revolution. Iran provides refuge to about 2 million Afghans, though it has refused to accept more in recent years and, indeed, tried to force many to repatriate.

Following the emergence of the Taliban and their harsh treatment of Afghanistan's Shi'a minority, Iran stepped up assistance to the Northern Alliance. Relations with the Taliban deteriorated further in 1998 after Taliban forces seized the Iranian consulate in Mazari Sharif and executed Iranian diplomats, who were accused of being secret spies. Following this incident, Iran almost went to war with the Taliban by massing up troops and tanks on the border with Afghanistan.

As a response, the Taliban immediately began gathering and recruiting great number of men along the border with

Iran. Many foreign fighters from Pakistan and Arab nations were also arriving. Iranian politicians decided to call it off because Afghans are known to raid cities and loot them, a similar event that occurred in early 1700s when all major Iranian cities were sacked and huge numbers of Iranians killed. This as well as intervention by the United Nations Security Council and the United States prevented an imminent Iranian war with the Taliban. Since 2001, the new government has engaged in cordial relations with both Iran and the United States, even as relations between the two countries have grown strained due to American objections to Iran's nuclear program. Relations very recently in 2007 and 2008 grew when Iran donated much aid to Afghan infrastructure and Afghan President Hamid Karzai vowed to stand by his ally, Ahmadinejad. Most of the Afghan people support the Iranian government and most Iranians wish to see Afghanistan develop. In fact, the two nations have stated they wish to create a trade league in an effort to improve standards. Iran has also declared their support for the Afghan Republic in the tense Afghan-Pakistani stiff drop in relations.

With Russia

In the nineteenth century, Afghanistan served as a strategic buffer state between Czarist Russian and the British Empire in the subcontinent. Afghanistan's relations with Moscow became more cordial after the Bolshevik Revolution in 1917. The Soviet Union was the first country to establish diplomatic relations with Afghanistan after the Third Anglo-Afghan war and signed an Afghan-Soviet nonaggression pact in 1921, which also provided for Afghan transit rights through the Soviet Union. Early Soviet assistance included financial aid, aircraft and attendant technical personnel, and telegraph operators. The Soviets began a major economic assistance program in Afghanistan in the 1950s. Between 1954 and 1978, Afghanistan received more than $1 billion in Soviet aid, including substantial military assistance. In 1973, the two countries announced a $200-million assistance agreement on gas and oil development, trade, transport, irrigation, and factory construction. Following the 1979 invasion, the Soviets augmented their large aid commitments to shore up the Afghan economy and rebuild the Afghan military. They provided the Karmal regime an unprecedented $800 million. The Soviet Union supported the Najibullah regime even after the withdrawal of Soviet troops in February 1989.

Today, unresolved questions concerning Soviet MIA/POWs in Afghanistan remain an issue between Russia and Afghanistan. Tajik rebels based in Afghanistan in July 1993 attacked a Russian border outpost in Tajikistan, killing 25 Russians and prompting Russian retaliatory strikes, which caused extensive damage in northern Afghanistan. Reports of Afghan support for the Tajik rebels led to cool relations between the two countries. Russia became increasingly disenchanted with the Taliban over their support for Chechen rebels and for providing a sanctuary for terrorist groups active in Central Asia and in Russia itself. Russia provided military assistance to the Northern Alliance, who eventually proved a major force in the efforts to overthrow the Taliban regime following U.S. intervention in 2001. In October 2005, Russian defense officials stated they will be giving helicopters and other military equipment to Afghanistan's army worth US $30 million.

With India

It is remarkable, that India has traditionally enjoyed good relations with the Afghan government. Historically, the region was tied to the civilization of South Asia, and the ancient Hindu kingdom of Gandhara may have covered what is now the Kabul province. President Hamid Karzai graduated from a university in India. Despite that, India supported the Soviet invasion and occupation of Afghanistan. It also supported the Afghan Northern Alliance "unofficially" against the Taliban. Relations deteriorated after the Taliban took power. During the course of the hijack of Indian Airlines Flight 814, the Taliban requested recognition by India in exchange for help in negotiations.

The request was not acted upon by the Indian Government. After the fall of the Taliban, India resumed previous ties. India has donated buses, aircraft and has imparted training to its fledgling police force. During President Hamid Karzai's visit to New Delhi, Indian Prime Minister Manmohan Singh pledged an additional $50 million in assistance to Afghanistan, bringing the total Indian pledge to $650 million — of which $200 million has already been spent. India is also reconstructing a road in the remote southwestern Afghan province of Nimroz. The project is being carried out by state-owned Border Roads Organization (BRO), the mission statement of which states that the BRO is India's "most reputed, multifaceted, transnational, modern construction organization committed to meeting the strategic needs of the armed forces." The killing of a BRO employee by the neo-Taliban in November 2005 prompted the Indian authorities to dispatch approximately 200 Indo-Tibetan Border Police commandos to Afghanistan in March 2006 to provide security for Indians working in various construction projects in the country.

With United States of America

Notably, relations with the United States can be traced back to over 150 years, to the early 1800s, when the first recorded person from America was visiting Afghanistan.

In fact, the 1940s, the United States established its first official embassy in Kabul. The first U.S. Ambassador to Afghanistan was Cornelius Van Engert. The first official Afghanistan Ambassador to the United States was Habibullah Khan Tarzi who served from 1948 to 1953. Since the 1950s the U.S. extended an economic assistance program focused on the development of Afghanistan's physical infrastructure which included roads, dams, and power plants. Later, U.S. aid shifted from infrastructure projects to technical assistance programs to help develop the skills needed to build a modern economy. Dwight D. Eisenhower visited Kabul in December 1959, becoming the first U.S. President to travel to Afghanistan. The Peace Corps was active in Afghanistan between 1962 and 1979. During the early 1960s former King of Afghanistan, Zahir Shah, visited the United States and met with John F. Kennedy. After the April 1978 coup, relations deteriorated. In February 1979, U.S. Ambassador Adolph "Spike" Dubs was murdered in Kabul after security forces burst in on his kidnappers. The U.S. then reduced bilateral assistance and terminated a small military training program.

All remaining assistance agreements were ended after the Soviet invasion of Afghanistan. Following the Soviet invasion, the United States supported diplomatic efforts to achieve a Soviet withdrawal. In addition, generous U.S. contributions to the refugee program in Pakistan played a major part in efforts to assist Afghans in need. U.S. efforts also included helping Afghans living inside Afghanistan.

This cross-border humanitarian assistance program aimed at increasing Afghan self-sufficiency and helping Afghans resist Soviet attempts to drive civilians out of the rebel-dominated countryside. During the period of Soviet occupation of Afghanistan, the U.S. provided about 3 billion

US dollars in military and economic assistance to the Afghan Mujahideens. Following the September 11 attacks, the United States launched an attack on the Taliban government as part of Operation Enduring Freedom. Following the overthrow of the Taliban, the U.S. supported the new government of Afghanistan and continues to station thousands of U.S. troops in the country. Their aim is to help the new government of President Hamid Karzai establish authority all across Afghanistan and hunt down insurgents that are launching attacks. Afghanistan supported the 2003 Invasion of Iraq.

The United States is also the leading nation in the rebuilding or reconstruction of Afghanistan. It has been providing multi-billion US dollars in weapons and aid, as well as infrastructure development. In 2005, the United States and Afghanistan signed a strategic partnership agreement committing both nations to a long-term relationship. U.S. President George W. Bush and First Lady Laura Bush made a surprise visit to Afghanistan on March 1, 2006. Hamid Karzai is hailed as an example of a great leader by most U.S. politicians, universities and media outlets everytime he visits the USA.

With Germany

The German-Afghan relationship is long and has been mostly cordial. Many Afghan academics studied in Germany, many more sought refuge in Germany during the years of civil war. There has been significant cultural exchange over the years. Several of the best secondary schools in Kabul are founded and supported by the German government. Germany remains one of the most significant donors of foreign aid and partners in the rebuilding of Afghanistan. The Bonn agreement for the post Taliban governance of Afghanistan was debated and signed in the former seat of government of Western Germany.

United Nations

During the Soviet occupation, the United Nations was highly critical of the U.S.S.R.'s interference in the internal affairs of Afghanistan and was instrumental in obtaining a negotiated Soviet withdrawal under the terms of the Geneva Accords. In the aftermath of the Accords and subsequent Soviet withdrawal, the United Nations has assisted in the repatriation of refugees and has provided humanitarian aid such as health care, educational programs, and food and has supported mine-clearing operations. The UNDP and associated agencies have undertaken a limited number of development projects. However, the UN reduced its role in Afghanistan in 1992 in the wake of fierce factional strife in and around Kabul.

The UN Secretary General has designated a personal representative to head the Office for the Coordination of Humanitarian Assistance to Afghanistan (UNOCHA) and the Special Mission to Afghanistan (UNSMA), both based in Islamabad, Pakistan. Throughout the late 1990s, 2000, and 2001, the UN unsuccessfully strived to promote a peaceful settlement between the Afghan factions as well as provide humanitarian aid, this despite increasing Taliban restrictions upon UN personnel and agencies.

4

Foreign Relations of Pakistan

Pakistan is a South Asian country located in the mountainous region adjoining Central Asia and the Middle East. It has a 1,046 kilometre (650 mile) coastline along the Arabian Sea and Gulf of Oman in the south, and is bordered by Afghanistan and Iran in the west, the Republic of India in the east and the People's Republic of China in the far northeast. Tajikistan also lies adjacent to Pakistan but is separated by the narrow Wakhan Corridor. In recent times, Pakistan has been called part of the New Middle East. The region forming modern Pakistan was home to the ancient Indus Valley Civilisation and then, successively, recipient of ancient Vedic, Persian, Turco-Mongol, Indo-Greek and Islamic cultures. The area has witnessed invasions and/or settlement by the Aryans, Persians, Greeks, Arabs, Turks, Afghans, Mongols and the British. It was a part of British India during the British Raj from 1858 to 1947, until the Indian independence movement led by Mahatma Gandhi. When the Pakistan Movement for a state for Muslims, led by Muhammad Ali Jinnah and the Muslim League resulted in the independence and creation of the state of Pakistan, that comprised the provinces of Sindh, North-West Frontier Province, West Punjab, Balochistan and East Bengal. With the adoption of its constitution in 1956, Pakistan became an Islamic republic. In 1971, a civil war in East Pakistan resulted in intervention from India and the subsequent independence of Bangladesh. Pakistan's history has been characterized by periods of economic growth, military rule and political instability.

BASIC FACTS	
Capital	Islamabad
Largest city	Karachi
Official languages	Urdu, English
Other languages	Punjabi, Pashto, Sindhi, Seraiki, Balochi
Government	Semi-presidential federal democratic republic
– President	Asif Ali Zardari (PPP)
– Formation	
– Independence	from the British Empire
– Declared	14 August 1947
– Islamic republic	23 March 1956
Area	
– Total	803,940 km2 (36th) 340,403 sq mi
– Water (%)	3.1
Population	
– 2008 estimate	165,900,000 (6th)
– 1998 census	132,352,279
GDP (PPP)	2008 estimate
– Total	$439.558 billion
– Per capita	$2,738
HDI (2008)	0.562 (medium) (139th)
Currency	Pakistani Rupee (Rs.) (PKR)

Pakistan is the second largest Muslim country in terms of population (behind Indonesia), and its status as a declared nuclear power, being the only Islamic nation to have that status, plays a part in its international role. Pakistan is also an important member of the Organisation of the Islamic Conference (OIC).

Pakistan is an active member of the United Nations. Historically, its foreign policy has encompassed difficult relations with the India; especially on the core-issue of Kashmir, over which it has fought 3 wars, a desire for a stable Afghanistan, long-standing close relations with China, closer cultural and economic ties with Iran, extensive security and economic interests in the Persian Gulf and wide-ranging bilateral relations with the United States and other Western countries.

Wary of Soviet expansion, Pakistan had strong relations with both the United States of America and the People's Republic of China during much of the Cold War.

It was a member of the CENTO and SEATO military alliances. Its alliance with the USA was especially close after the Soviets invaded the neighbouring country of Afghanistan. In 1964, Pakistan signed the Regional Cooperation for Development (RCD) Pact with Turkey and Iran, when all three countries were closely allied with the U.S., and as neighbors of the Soviet Union, wary of perceived Soviet expansionism. To this day, Pakistan has a close relationship with Turkey. RCD became defunct after the Iranian Revolution, and a Pakistani-Turkish initiative led to the founding of the Economic Cooperation Organisation (ECO) in 1985. Pakistan's relations with India have improved recently and this has opened up Pakistan's foreign policy to issues beyond security. This development might completely change the complexion of Pakistan's foreign relations.

Bilateral Relations

With Azerbaijan

Pakistan recognized independence of Azerbaijan 1991

(the second country after Turkey) and the two countries established diplomatic relations in 1992. Pakistan was one of the first countries to open its Embassy in Baku.

With People's Republic of China

In 1950, Pakistan was among the first countries to break relations with the Republic of China or Taiwan and recognize the People's Republic of China. Following the Sino-Indian hostilities of 1962, Pakistan's relations with the PRC became stronger; since then, the two countries have regularly exchanged high-level visits resulting in a variety of agreements. China has provided economic, military, and technical assistance to Pakistan.

The alliance remains strong. Favorable relations with China have been a pillar of Pakistan's foreign policy. China strongly supported Pakistan's opposition to Soviet involvement in Afghanistan and was perceived by Pakistan as a regional counterweight to India and the USSR.

The PRC and Pakistan also share a close military relation, with China supplying a range of modern armaments to the Pakistani defence forces. Lately, military cooperation has deepened with joint projects producing armaments ranging from fighter jets to guided missile frigates. Chinese cooperation with Pakistan has reached high economic points with substantial investment from China in Pakistani infrastructural expansion.

With India

Since independence, relations between Pakistan and India have been characterized by rivalry and suspicion. Although many issues divide the two countries, the most sensitive one since independence has been the status of Kashmir.

At the time of independence and the departure of the British from South Asia, the princely state of Kashmir, though ruled by a Hindu Maharajah installed by the British colonialists, had an overwhelmingly Muslim population. When the Maharajah hesitated in acceding to either Pakistan or India in 1947, his Muslim subjects, aided by Pashtun tribesmen from Pakistan, revolted in favor of joining Pakistan. India has long alleged that regular troops from Pakistan had participated in the partial occupation of Kashmir from the Western front,.

Under pressure to quell the invasion by armed tribals, the Maharaja offered his allegiance to secular India. Indian troops occupied the central & eastern portion of Kashmir, including its capital, Srinagar, while the west-north western parts were occupied by Pakistan.

India addressed this dispute in the United Nations on January 1, 1948. One year later, the UN arranged a cease-fire along a line dividing Kashmir, but leaving the northern end of the line undemarcated and the vale of Kashmir (with the majority of the population) under Indian occupation. India and Pakistan agreed with UN resolutions which called for a UN-supervised plebiscite to determine the state's future. India and Pakistan have since refused to carry out the plebiscite and refused to remove their estimated 700,000 troops, one of the highest density of troops to civilian population in the world, from the region.

Full-scale hostilities erupted in September 1965, when insurgents who were trained and supplied by Pakistan were operating in Kashmir. Hostilities ceased three weeks later, following mediation efforts by the UN and interested countries. In January 1966, Indian and Pakistani representatives met in Tashkent, U.S.S.R., and agreed to attempt a peaceful settlement of Kashmir and their other differences.

Following the Indo-Pakistani War of 1971 when India took advantage of civil disturbances in Pakistan's east wing and aided the separatist Bengali's to achieve independence, Bengladesh was located almost 1000 km away from the mainland of Pakistan, Pakistan President Zulfiqar Ali Bhutto and Indian Prime Minister Indira Gandhi met in Shimla, India, in July 1972 for the Shimla Accords. They agreed to a line of control in Kashmir resulting from the December 17, 1971 cease-fire, and endorsed the principle of settlement of bilateral disputes through peaceful means. In 1974, Pakistan and India agreed to resume postal and telecommunications linkages, and to enact measures to facilitate travel. Trade and diplomatic relations were restored in 1976 after a hiatus of five years.

Much to Pakistan and the world communities surprise, India's nuclear test in 1974 generated great uncertainty in Pakistan and is generally acknowledged to have been the impetus for Pakistan's nuclear weapons development program. In 1983, the Pakistani and Indian governments accused each other of aiding separatists in their respective countries, i.e., Sikhs in India's Punjab state and Sindhis in Pakistan's Sindh province. In April 1984, tensions erupted after troops were deployed to the Siachen Glacier, a high-altitude desolate area close to the China border left undemarcated by the cease-fire agreement (Karachi Agreement) signed by Pakistan and India in 1949. Indian troops heightened tensions in the region by occupying several uninhabitable posts along the Siachen glacier.

Tensions diminished after Rajiv Gandhi became Prime Minister in November 1984 and after a group of Sikh hijackers were brought to trial by Pakistan in March 1985. In December 1985, President Zia and Prime Minister Rajiv Gandhi pledged not to attack each other's nuclear establishments. A formal "no attack" agreement was signed in January 1991. In early 1986, the Indian and Pakistani governments began high-level talks to resolve the Siachen Glacier border dispute and to improve trade.

Bilateral tensions increased in early 1990, when Kashmiri militants began a campaign of violence against Indian occupation of Kashmir. Their anti Hindu policies led to the genocide and migration of ethnic Hindu Minority Kashmiri Pundits. Subsequent high-level bilateral meetings relieved the tensions between India and Pakistan, but relations worsened again after terrorist bombings in Mumbai, in March 1993. Talks between the Foreign Secretaries of both countries in January 1994 resulted in deadlock.

In the late 1990s, the Indo-Pakistani relationship veered sharply between rapprochement and conflict. After taking office in February 1997, Prime Minister Nawaz Sharif moved to resume an official dialogue with India. A number of meetings at the foreign secretary and Prime Ministerial level took place, with positive atmospherics but little concrete progress. The relationship improved markedly when Indian Prime Minister Vajpayee traveled to Lahore for a summit with Sharif in February 1999. There was considerable hope that the meeting could lead to a breakthrough. Unfortunately, in spring 1999 infiltrators from Pakistan occupied positions on the Indian side of the Line of Control in the remote, mountainous area of Kashmir near Kargil, thereby threatening the ability of India to supply its forces on the Siachen Glacier. By early summer, serious fighting flared in the Kargil sector. The fighting lasted about a month and Indian forces were able to push back the infiltrators Indian Army left their posts in winter. The Pakistan Prime Minister Nawaz Sharif under pressure from the US president Bill Clinton withdrew Pakistan's army from remaining posts.

Relations between India and Pakistan continued to be strained when Pervez Musharraf came to power on October 12, 1999 Pakistani coup d'état. India alleged that Pakistan provided monetary and material support to Kashmiri militants, a charge which Pakistan has always denied.

In 2001, following the 9/11 attacks, the United States formed an alliance with Pakistan in its War on Terror against Afghanistan and preferring to confer on Pakistan the title of *Major Non-NATO Ally*. Pakistanis themselves started to grow disillusioned with jihadi militants, regardless of the causes they claimed to follow. Musharraf dropped his insistence that no issues could be discussed until the Kashmir issue was fully solved. Bilateral meetings between the two sides resulted in new people-to-people contacts. Air services and cricket matches were restored. Trains started plying between Sindh and Rajasthan. Bans on Indian movies and TV channels were eased in Pakistan. Transport links across the Line of Control in Kashmir were re-opened. More importantly the intelligence services and armies of the two countries started to cooperate in identifying terrorists who threatened attacks. On June 20, 2004, both countries agreed to extend a nuclear testing ban and to set up a hotline between their foreign secretaries aimed at preventing misunderstandings that might lead to a nuclear war. In 2007 the two countries agreed to start flights between their capitals. Legal trade between the countries reached 2 billion dollars per year.

With Afghanistan

Geographically, Pakistan shares a long and porous

border with Afghanistan named as the Durand Line. The border is poorly marked. The problem is exacerbated by cultural, historical, linguistic, ethnic and political ties crossing close relations between peoples who live on both sides of the border. This is further complicated by the fact that many of the Pashtun tribes on both sides of the border are often married and refuse to recognize it.

Following the Soviet invasion of Afghanistan in 1979, the Pakistani Government played a vital role in supporting the Afghan resistance movement and assisting Afghan refugees. Pakistan absorbed an estimated 5 million refugees and provided shelter, education, food rations and assistance to them. Social and health indicators dropped considerably during this period as Polio and Tuberculosis, previously eradicated from the country, were re-introduced and the country became awashed with drugs, weapons, prostitution rings and increased incidences of crime, poverty and violence.

After the Soviet withdrawal in February 1989, Pakistan, with cooperation from the world community, continued to provide extensive support for displaced Afghans. In 1999, the United States provided approximately $70 million in humanitarian assistance to Afghanistan and Afghan refugees in Pakistan, mainly through multilateral organizations and NGOs.

Pakistani strategists view Afghanistan as providing "strategic depth" in the event of a war with neighboring India. In the event that the Indian Army crosses into Pakistan, the Pakistan Army would temporary locate supplies in Afghanistan and prepare for a counter-offensive. Furthermore, many Pakistani saw in Afghanistan and Afghans a common bond based on religion, history, culture, language and ethnic ties.

At various times, Pakistan backed the mujahideen against the Soviets, mujahideen against each other and the Taliban against the Northern Alliance. The overthrow of the Taliban Regime in November 2001 has seen somewhat strained relations between Afghanistan and Pakistan. The present Karzai administration in Kabul feels that the remnants of the former Taliban government are being supported by factions within Pakistan for the same above reasons. Interestingly, Hamid Karzai's parents both lived in Pakistan during the Soviet occupation of Afghanistan. However, Pakistan has said the government cannot control all elements of its intelligence agency, the ISI, which Afghanistan, Iran and several Western countries accuse of contributing to instability.

On June 15th 2008, in the aftermath of successful major Taliban operations, due to growing internal instability within Afghanistan and the Karzai's government inability to address domestic issues, the Afghan government issued a statement threatening to send its army across the Durand Line in pursuit of rebels stationed along the mountainous border inside Pakistan; the statement caused considerable damage to bilateral relations and was rebuked by Pakistani officials as inappropriate.

The United States, however, has stated it does support a temporary Afghan invasion of rogue tribal areas in Pakistan if the Pakistani army is incapable of doing so. The fall of the Taliban regime has made Afghan - Indian relations considerably stronger. India has invested in many transport projects in Afghanistan.

Indian officials claim that Pakistan's ISI had a major hand in the Indian Embassy bombing in Kabul. This claim has been supported and confirmed by the Afghan

Government. A large share of Afghanistan's foreign and economic trade is either with, originates from or passes through, Pakistan. Afghanistan is largely dependent on Pakistan for basic foodstuffs and most of its commerce has been directed towards Pakistan.

However, improved relations with Iran, Afghanistan's cultural neighbor, the country has found more trade routes besides Pakistan. This also contributes to worse relations as the government tries finding ways to lessen its connections with Pakistan and find more markets to trade with, mainly Iran and its Northern allies.

With Tajikistan

Geographically Tajikistan is the nearest Central Asian State to Pakistan - fourteen kilometeres between two countries. Pakistan established diplomatic relationship with the Republic of Tajikistan in 1992, but cooperation between these two countries started from 1991.

With Sri Lanka

Sri Lanka's ties with Pakistan is warming gradually. Pakistan has been recently supplying military equipment to the Sri Lankan armed forces. Pakistan is against and does not support the Tamil rebels.

With Bangladesh

The Bangladesh-Pakistan relationship is yet to be at a level that may be called warm. However since full diplomatic relations were implemented in January 1976, it has shown improvement in bilateral relations concerning commerce, culture and trade and making reconciliatory agreements.

The following are the major landmarks in their reconciliation:

(1) An August 1973 agreement between Bangladesh and Pakistan on the repatriation of numerous individuals, including 90,000 Pakistani prisoners of war stranded in Bangladesh as a result of the 1971 conflict;

(2) A February 1974 accord by Bangladesh and Pakistan on mutual diplomatic recognition, followed more than 2 years later by establishment of formal diplomatic relations on January 18th 1976.

(3) The organization by the UN High Commissioner for Refugees (UNHCR) of an airlift that moved almost 250,000 Bengalis from Pakistan to Bangladesh, and non-Bengalis from Bangladesh to Pakistan; and

(4) Exchanges of high-level visits, including a visit by Prime Minister Benazir Bhutto to Bangladesh in 1989 and visits by Prime Minister Khaleda Zia to Pakistan in 1992 and in 1995.

The main issues yet to be resolved are:

(a) Division of assets from the pre-1971 period

(b) Repatriation of 250,000 ethnic Biharis known as "Stranded Pakistanis".

(c) Possibly the most important and most sensitive issue is the Question of Pakistan's apology for the genocide in 1971 which has lead to the break down of numerous talks between the two.

With Iraq

Iraq and Pakistan have had close cultural, friendly, and cooperative relations since the latter's independence in 1947. Issues such as Iraqi support for Pakistan in its 1971 war with India (which Iraq also has excellent relations with), and Pakistani support for Iraq against Iran in the Iran-Iraq War have forged relations between the two. Relations soured during the Gulf War when Pakistan contributed troops for the UN Coalition, seeing it as a betrayal due to Iraq's constant support for Pakistan in their previous wars with India. In 2002, Saddam Hussein visited India and said he gave his unwavering support to India over the Kashmir dispute. In 2003, Pakistan rejected US's request to send troops for the invasion which have helped soothed relations between the two.

WWith Israel

Pakistan has stated it will not recognize the State of Israel until a Palestine nation-state is created and Palestinian refugees return to their home lands. Afterwards, Pakistan would consider the relations between Tel Aviv-Yafo (the U.N. Recognized capital city) and Islamabad.

In 2003, President Pervez Musharraf raised the issue of possible diplomatic relations with Israel, and in 2005 the foreign ministers of the two countries held talks for the first time. However, following the meeting Musharraf said Pakistan will not recognise the state of Israel until an independent Palestinian state is established.

With Kyrgyz Republic

Formally, Pakistan extended diplomatic recognition to the Kyrgyz Republic on December 20, 1991. A Protocol for the establishment of diplomatic relations between Pakistan and Kyrgyzstan was signed on May 10, 1992. Pakistan's diplomatic resident Mission at Ambassadorial level was established at Bishkek in August 1995. There have been high level visits from both sides in last ten years. In December 2000, the Chief Executive of Pakistan extended an invitation to Kyrgyz President Askar Akayev to pay a State visit to Pakistan. The invitation was accepted by the President of Kyrgyzstan.

Further Pakistan and Kyrgyzstan co-operate with each other in various fields for the promotion of trade and economic relations between the two countries. A few Pakistan nationals have established their business concerns in the fields of hoteling, pharmacy and tourism in Kyrgyz Republic.

During the visit of Minister of State for Economic Affairs in December 1991, an export credit of US$ 10 million was offered to Kyrgyzstan for the establishment of pharmaceutical factory at Bishkek. An agreement was signed in May 1993. On the request of Kyrgyzstan, keeping in view of friendly and brotherly relations with Kyrgyzstan, the Government of Pakistan rescheduled the loan repayment and prolonged its payment for the next six years. An agreement on rescheduling was signed accordingly.

One of the achievements in the economic cooperation between the two countries is the opening of the branch of the National Bank of Pakistan at Bishkek. The main aim of the bank is to boost the trade and economic relations between Pakistan and Kyrgyzstan. The National Bank of Kyrgyzstan took a decision to issue the license for the branch of the National Bank of Pakistan to open the accounts for local individuals from January 1, 2002. Earlier, the National Bank of Pakistan was authorized to open the accounts for the companies and organizations only. Within one year after the opening, this branch has become the profit-earning unit. After some time, the bank would be able to extend small credit facility to the local population. The National Bank of Pakistan has also offered a regular training programme for the Kyrgyz Bankers. Pakistan is extending all possible help for Kyrgyz nationals under the Technical Assistance programme in the field of education, diplomacy, banking, English language and postal services, etc.

The leadership of the Kyrgyz Republic has demonstrated keen interest to have more bilateral cultural cooperation and people to people contact by establishing sister city relationship with the cities of Kyrgyzstan and Pakistan. Establishment of sister city relationships between Quetta-Bishkek and Osh-Sialkot are under consideration by the two sides.

Both the countries have expressed their desire to conclude a Cultural Agreement with the aim of developing relations and mutual understanding between Pakistan and Kyrgyzstan. A draft Cultural Agreement is under consideration. A draft Agreement between APP and "Kabar" news agency of Kyrgyzstan is also under consideration.

Being the members of OIC and ECO, Pakistan and Kyrgyzstan support each other on various global and regional issues as well as during the elections to the key posts in the international organizations.

With Turkmenistan

Notably, Pakistan was one of the first countries to recognize Turkmenistan as an independent country in December 1991. Pakistan established formal diplomatic relations with Turkmenistan on 10th May 1992. The two countries enjoy close and cordial relations which are rooted in common history, culture and traditions.

Exchange of high-level visits during the last 10 years give credence to the fact that Pakistan and Turkmenistan have laid foundation of mutually beneficial relations, friendship and understanding. The hallmark of the friendship was demonstrated during the official visit of the Chief Executive of Pakistan to Ashgabat in May - 2000, and again during his brief stop-over in November 2000. In the short span of 10 years, there have been six visits of Head of State/Head of Government from Pakistan to Turkmenistan. President of Turkmenistan Saparmurate Niyazov had visited Pakistan thrice in August 1994, March 1995 and March 1997.

So far, two countries have signed 21 Agreements and Memoranda of understanding in the fields of oil and gas, transport, energy, trade, science and culture. The issuance of commemorative stamps by Pakistan will be an important milestone in the gamut of bilateral relations.

With Lebanon

In fact, Lebanon and Pakistan have good relations. Pakistan has also been a steadfast supporter of Lebanon particularly when it was invaded by its southern neighbour. Additionally, Pakistan has extended moral, diplomatic and material support to Lebanon and refuses to recognize Israel officially, as a legitimate country in solidarity with the Palestinian, Lebanese and other Middle Eastern countries. Trade between the two countries has been growing considerably in recent years and has helped Lebanon rebuild itself after years of war.

Many Pakistani skilled professionals and doctors have gone to Lebanon to help the people and Pakistan has opened up seats in many of its university to accommodate Lebanese students wishing to partake in higher studies. Due to the popularity of Arabic in Pakistan, Lebanese music, television shows, cultural shows and cuisine are popular and widespread throughout the country.

With United Arab Emirates

It is remarkable that Pakistan was the first country to accord formal recognition to UAE on its achieving independence. Bilateral relations and mutually beneficial cooperation have progressed steadily since then.

Pakistan and the UAE enjoy extremely close and traternal relations, founded on deep-rooted cultural affinities, shared faith and traditions, as also geographic proximity and identity of interests. These relations date back to the UAE's formation in 1971, and have since evolved into wide-ranging co-operation in various fields.

UAE has been a major donor of economic assistance to Pakistan. UAE has been appreciative of Pakistan's contribution to the evolution of key institutions in the Emirates such as armed forces, police, health and education, and has reciprocated in the same friendly manner to the full satisfaction of Pakistan. The two countries have common perceptions on all international and regional issues of mutual concern. Frequent exchanges of high level visits and regular bilateral consultations between the two countries are reflective of the fact that Pakistan and UAE have laid strong foundations of mutually beneficial relations, friendship and peaceful cooperation over the years, UAE has emerged as one of Pakistan's major economic and trading partners. A large number of Pakistani expatriates, numbering nearly 400,000 are gainfully employed in UAE. The Pakistani expatriates in UAE have contributed in a significant manner to promotion of bilateral understanding and to the economy of Pakistan through their home remittances.

With Iran

Historically, Iran was the first nation to recognize Pakistan. Since then, Pakistan has had close geopolitical and cultural-religious linkages with Iran. Relations between the two countries have existed since ancient times when the Pakistani region was part of the large Persian Empire. Persian is still considered the cultural language of Pakistan and most of Pakistan's national anthem is written in that language. Persian was the *lingua franca* of Pakistan up to 1843 when the British annexed parts of Pakistan and abolished its use in favour of Urdu and English.

Relations between Iran and Pakistan peaked in the 60's and 70's under the Shah with considerable joint ventures and assistance provided by Iran to Pakistan. Iran is also a popular tourist spot for Pakistan's Muslims, notably its Shia population which represents about 15% of Pakistan population of 170 million people. Low period have occurred, however, strains in the relationship appeared in the 1980s, when Pakistan and Iran supported opposing factions in the Afghan conflict. Also, some Pakistanis suspect Iranian support for the sectarian violence which has plagued Pakistan.

Furthermore, many Pakistanis were disappointed when much of Iran's nuclear research was stated as having originated from Pakistan, this despite the fact that Iran's nuclear program was started some 20 years before that of Pakistan's. Nevertheless, Pakistan pursues an active diplomatic relationship with Iran, including recent overtures to seek a negotiated settlement between Afghanistan's warring factions. Pakistan also supports Iran's use of Nuclear Technology for peaceful purposes. Both countries are endeavouring to improve and strengthen bilateral trade and commerce between them. On January 27th 2006, Pakistan, Iran, and India agreed to start work on IPI gasline which Pakistan needs to shrink the gap of demand and supply of energy in Pakistan to maintain economic growth. India has consistently stalled the talks asking for more time under the duress of the United States, but Pakistan and Iran have agreed to go ahead with the project even if India doesn't participate thus highlighting the two countries commitment to the project. Relations, however, once again have become strained over the ongoing Afghan conflict.

The Afghan Republic has consistently accused Pakistan's intelligence of supporting insurgents and contributing to an unstable Afghanistan. President Ahmadinejad vowed on an official visit to Kabul to stand by its cultural traditional neighbor at "all times, even when facing confusion from neighbors."

With Saudi Arabia

Kingdom of Saudi Arabia has helped Pakistan in many fields since Pakistan gained independence in 1947. Since the inception of Pakistan, Saudi Arabia has provided Pakistan with assistance in the form of fuel credit, fuel donation, loans, aid, donations, and gifts. Most famous example of Saudi Arabia's relationship with Pakistan is the Faisal Mosque, the National Mosque of the country in Islamabad, Pakistan. More recently, Saudi Arabia has given Pakistan hundreds of millions of dollars as a donation for the 2005 Earthquake in Pakistan. In fact, the Kingdom of Saudi Arabia was the number 1 donor, having contributed US $600 million.

Other forms of assistance given by Saudi Arabia include providing employment to millions of Pakistanis over the past 60 years. This has been a blessing for Pakistan in disguise as the workers who worked in Saudi Arabia not only accumulated wealth, when they came back to Pakistan, they led Pakistan's construction boom and introduction of modern goods and items. Saudi Arabia has also actively promoted Pakistan's social life by funding many social projects like building of Islamic community centres, relief foundations, and mosques throughout Pakistan.

Due to the Kingdom's continuing generosity, many places in Pakistan are named after Saudi Kings and Saudi Arabia in general. For example, the historic city previously named Lyallpur was renamed Faisalabad in honor of the late Faisal of Saudi Arabia. Also, in Karachi, Pakistan, there are neighbourhoods named Saud Colony, Saudabad, Faisal Colony. Also in Karachi, there is an airforce base name Faisal Airbase named after King Faisal and also, in the honor of King Faisal, the main business street of Pakistan is called Sharah-e-Faisal in Karachi. In 2005, due to passing of King Fahd of Saudi Arabia, Pakistan declared a three-day mourning period.

Saudi Arabia also hosted former Pakistani Prime Minister Nawaz Sharif for 8 years while he was in exile. During his stay there, Kingdom held talks with Sharif and even provided him with license to operate business in the Kingdom. It is believed that it was Kingdom of Saudi Arabia which held talks with President Pervez Musharraf of Pakistan to foster their relationship and to allow Sharif back in Pakistan. In March 2008, Saudi Arabia donated Pakistan US $300 million to over come the economic problems and crisis.

With Sultanate of Oman

The relationship between Muscat and Islamabad is warm, because it is the nearest Arab country to Pakistan. In 1958 Gwadar was part of Oman but was transferred to Pakistan in that year.

With North Korea

It is still not exactly clear when Pakistan opened

diplomatic ties to North Korea. It is said to be somewhere in the 1970s. Recent developments indicate that their relations were kept secretive to avoid suspicion from the west and the risk of economic sanctions.

With Japan

It is worth mentioning that despite having been through various phases and having witnessed some vicissitudes, Japan-Pakistan relations have kept growing to the mutual benefit of the two countries. Until the late 1950s, the relationship was essentially that of two developing countries. Pakistan, being the main source of raw cotton for Japan's textile industry, was one of its major trading partners. Japanese spindles on the other hand helped build Pakistan's textile industry. In the 1960s, Japan, however, re-emerged as a modern industrialized nation and started extending Yen loan assistance to Pakistan. The Japanese assistance was doubled to Pakistan following the Soviet invasion of Afghanistan.

Japan, since then, has been Pakistan's major source of economic assistance, a leading trading partner and an important source of foreign investment. Tokyo and Islamabad have long enjoyed cordial and formidable relations throughout chronology. Japan's economic assistance has played a very important role in the development of Pakistan's economic and social infrastructure. The major projects, which have been funded by the Government of Japan, include the Indus Highway Project, a number of power projects in various provinces of Pakistan, Rural Roads Construction Project and the Children Hospital PIMS Islamabad Project.

Presently the Kohat Tunnel Project and the Ghazi Brotha Dam Project are being completed with the help of the Japanese assistance. There has been a regular exchange of high level visits between the two countries. Pakistan and Japan had established formal diplomatic relations on 28th April 1952. The 50th anniversary of the establishment of diplomatic relations, jointly celebrated by the two countries in 2002, was a significant landmark in the history of this friendship.

With Vietnam

Vietnam and Pakistan officially established diplomatic relations on 8 November 1972. Pakistan opened its Embassy in Hanoi in 1973. However, due to economic reasons, Pakistan closed the embassy in 1980. Vietnam also opened its embassy in Islamabad in 1978 and had to close it down in 1984 due to its own economic difficulty. Bilateral relations between Vietnam and Pakistan in recent years have considerably improved. Both countries leaders expressed their willingness to strengthen their existing relations, not only in the political sphere but also in other areas such as trade and economics, and exchange more visits from one to another's country, including both high-ranking and working visits.

Pakistan reopened its embassy in Hanoi in October 2000. Vietnam also reopened its embassy in Islamabad in December 2005 and trade office in Karachi in November 2005.

With Arab Republic of Egypt

Pakistan and Egypt, both being Muslim countries, share cordial relations. Both are also members of the OIC (Oraganization of Islamic Conference), as well as "the next eleven" and "D8".

With Sudan

Due to both states sharing the same religion, being

former British colonies, and refusing to recognize Israel as a legitimate nation, Pakistan and Sudan have shared generally close warm relations for decades, these relations strengthened when Sudan supported Pakistan in the Indo-Pakistani Wars. But because of certain issues however, such as Pakistan's strong relations with the United States, and friendly Sudanese relations with India, Iran, and Bangladesh, things between the two countries have reached a boiling point. Despite this tension, relations between the two nations can be considered amicable.

With France

Pakistan and France have high levels of diplomatic meetings and are in good terms with one another. However, these good relations haven't been around very long due to France's relations with Pakistans rival; India. Things are improving much between Pakistan and France and France donates large funds to help Pakistan with its economic problems.

With Soviet Union/Russian Federation

Both Pakistan and Russia established diplomatic relations on 1 May 1948. However, relations between these two countries have been strained in the past, because of the Soviet Union's and Russia's closeness to India, and because of Pakistan's support for the Afghan rebels during the invasion by the USSR.

With Turkey

Remarkably, the relations between Pakistan and Turkey are a rare example of good relations between two countries in the broader Middle East. The relationship between the two countries and their people is based on centuries of a shared history, culture, civilization and faith. In Pakistan, the founder of modern Turkey, Mustafa Ataturk, is regarded as a hero. Kemal Atatürk's triumph in forging a strong and progressive Turkey was seen by many of the Muslims of the South Asia as an embodiment of their national aspirations and served as an inspiration during their struggle for independence, which culminated in the emergence of Pakistan as an independent nation in 1947.

Most conservative Muslims continue to view Atatürk as the destroyer of the Caliphate; this resulted in the Khalifat movement in the South Asia in the 1920s and in the pan-Islamic rhetoric of present-day Sunni jihadi groups. There is a remarkable coalescence of views between Turkey and Pakistan on major issues of regional and global significance, particularly since both have been allied to the United States.

The two countries have always extended full support to each other on several issues. Pakistan fully supports the cause of the Turkish Cypriot people and Turkey has backed the cause of the people of Jammu and Kashmir. Their tensions over supporting rival factions during the Afghan civil war were reduced by the US-backed overthrow of the Taliban regime.

The two countries have also cooperated over the issue of Bosnia and Herzegovina and have adopted joint positions on this issue at the international fora. The prime ministers of the two countries took a joint trip to Sarajevo in 1993 to express solidarity with Bosnian Muslims. Both countries also sent peace-keeping forces to Bosnia. The two countries have worked closely with each other in the context of the Economic Cooperation Organization (ECO) as well.

Pakistan actively participated in the second ECO summit in Istanbul in July 1993. Similarly the Turkish delegation to the third ECO summit held in Islamabad in 1995, was led by President Demirel and extended full support to the strengthening of the important regional organization which includes all Central Asian countries and Azerbaijan.

The frequency of high level visits between Turkey and Pakistan has been one of the key factors in maintaining close ties between the two countries. Prime Minister of Pakistan Benazir Bhutto paid a three-day visit to Turkey in December 1993. President of Pakistan Sardar Farooq Khan Leghari also visited Turkey in September 1994. President of Turkey Suleyman Demirel paid a three-day official visit to Pakistan in 1995 and received a warm and enthusiastic welcome from the people of Pakistan. A number of agreements for increased cooperation between the two countries were signed during these visits.

In field of defence cooperation the commanders of the Armed Forces of the two countries exchange regular visits. There are regular programs of exchange of officers and training. The two countries have also purchased some defence related equipment from each other.

Similarly, in the field of economy and trade relations between the two countries have been somewhat limited. However over the last few years, both countries have made conscious and sustained efforts to improve their economic relations. The Turco-Pakistan Joint Economic Commission which meets at the ministerial level to strengthen economic relations, held its 10th session in Ankara in September 1995 and adopted a comprehensive protocol to promote economic and commercial cooperation between the two countries.

In the similar vein the 4th session of Turco-Pakistan Business Council was held in September 1995. There was also an exchange trade delegations between the two countries during 1995. As a result, bilateral trade between the two countries reached a level of more than $20 million in 1995. Cooperation between the private sectors of the two countries is on the increase. Some major contracts have been awarded to the Turkish companies such as STFA. Other Turkish companies are also planning to enter the large Pakistani market.

Cultural relations between Turkey and Pakistan are governed by a Cultural Cooperation Agreement. Specific cultural exchange programs are prepared under the agreement. The last protocol was signed in November 1992, for the years 1993-96. There have been a number of cultural exchange between the two countries which include visits of cultural troupes, participation in photographic, arts & crafts exhibitions and children's festivals. The Embassy of Pakistan in Ankara has also organized a number of cultural activities and Single Country Exhibitions to highlight the similarities and the diversity between the two cultures.

Radio and Television organizations of the two countries are working to establish closer relations. Turkey and Pakistan are cooperating in the field of education. This includes cooperation between the universities of the two countries; exchange of professors and scholars, holding of seminars, exhibitions and symposia and award of scholarships to the students of the two countries. The government of Pakistan has established Chairs of Urdu and Pakistan Studies at the Ankara and Istanbul Universities. Selcuk University is also operating a Department of Urdu with the help of a Pakistani teacher.

The determination of the two countries and their peoples to forge even closer links remains undiminished. While official rhetoric stresses "brotherly ties" between Pakistan and Turkey, there are some complications due to differences between secular Turkey and Pakistan's continuing slide to Islamic fundamentalism and extremism.

With Bosnia

Pakistan has close relations with Bosnia. Pakistan recognised their independence from Yugoslavia. Pakistan sent in UN Peacekeeping forces to the former Yugoslavia during the Yugoslav wars. Pakistan and Bosnia have a free trade agreement.

With United Kingdom & Commonwealth

Pakistan has been a member of the Commonwealth of Nations since independence in 1947. It was not a member of the British Commonwealth from 1972 until 1989, because of the Commonwealth's recognition of Bangladesh. It was readmitted to full membership of the Commonwealth in October 1989. It was suspended with the overthrow of the democratically elected government in 1999. Its full membership has been reinstated with the backing of the United Kingdom, Canada, Australia and New Zealand for Pakistan's support in the War on Terrorism. Pakistan maintains diplomatic relations with all Commonwealth countries even though it does not have its own High Commission in each capital.

With United States of America

Historically, no ally of the United States has faced as many sanctions from the US as Pakistan. The United States established diplomatic relations with Pakistan in 1949; reluctantly, at first. Since the Eisenhower administration, however, Pakistan and the US began developing more cozy relations. The American agreement to provide economic and military assistance to Pakistan and the latter's partnership in the Baghdad Pact, CENTO and SEATO strengthened relations between the two nations. At the time, its relationship with the U.S. was so close and friendly that it was called the United States' "most-allied ally" in Asia. Pakistanis felt betrayed and ill-compensated for the risks incurred in supporting the U.S. - after the U-2 Crisis of 1960, Soviet leader Nikita Khrushchev had threatened the nuclear annihilation of Pakistani cities. The U.S. suspension of military assistance during the 1965 Indo-Pakistan war generated a widespread feeling in Pakistan that the United States was not a reliable ally. Even though the United States suspended military assistance to both countries involved in the conflict, the suspension of aid affected Pakistan much more severely. Gradually, relations improved and arms sales were renewed in 1975. Then, in April 1979, the United States cut off economic assistance to Pakistan, except food assistance, as required under the Symington Amendment to the U.S. Foreign Assistance Act of 1961, due to concerns about Pakistan's nuclear program. The Soviet invasion of Afghanistan in December 1979 highlighted the common interest of Pakistan and the United States in peace and stability in South Asia.

In 1981, the United States and Pakistan agreed on a $3.2-billion military and economic assistance program aimed at helping Pakistan deal with the heightened threat to security in the region and its economic development needs. With U.S. assistance - in the largest covert operation in history - Pakistan armed and supplied anti-Soviet fighters in Afghanistan, eventually defeating the Soviets, who withdrew in 1988. Recognizing national security concerns and accepting Pakistan's assurances that it did not intend to construct a nuclear weapon, Congress waived restrictions (Symington Amendment) on military assistance to Pakistan.

In March 1986, the two countries agreed on a second

multi-year (FY 1988-93) $4-billion economic development and security assistance program. On October 1, 1990, however, the United States suspended all military assistance and new economic aid to Pakistan under the Pressler Amendment, which required that the President certify annually that Pakistan "does not possess a nuclear explosive device."

India's decision to conduct nuclear tests in May 1998 and Pakistan's matching response set back U.S. relations in the region, which had seen renewed U.S. Government interest during the second Clinton Administration. A presidential visit scheduled for the first quarter of 1998 was postponed and, under the Glenn Amendment, sanctions restricted the provision of credits, military sales, economic assistance, and loans to the government. An intensive dialogue on nuclear nonproliferation and security issues between Deputy Secretary Talbott and Foreign Secretary Shamshad Ahmad was initiated, with discussions focusing on CTBT signature and ratification, FMCT negotiations, export controls, and a nuclear restraint regime. The October 1999 overthrow of the democratically elected Sharif government triggered an additional layer of sanctions under Section 508 of the Foreign Appropriations Act which include restrictions on foreign military financing and economic assistance. U.S. Government assistance to Pakistan was limited mainly to refugee and counter-narcotics assistance.

It is remarkable that Pakistan moved decisively to ally itself with the United States in its war against Osama bin Laden and Al-Qaeda. It provided the U.S. a number of military airports and bases, for its attack on Afghanistan. It has arrested over five hundred Al-Qaeda members and handed them over to the United States; senior U.S. officers have been lavish in their praise of Pakistani efforts.

Since this strategic re-alignment towards U.S. policy, economic and military assistance has been flowing from the U.S. to Pakistan and sanctions have been lifted. In the three years before the attacks of September 11, Pakistan received approximately $9 million in American military aid. In the three years after, the number increased to $4.2 billion. In June 2004, President Bush designated Pakistan as a major non-NATO ally, making it eligible, among other things, to purchase advanced American military technology. In May, 2006, The Bush administration announced a major sale of missiles to Pakistan, valued at US $370 million.

International Disputes

- Status of Kashmir with the Republic of India.
- Durand line and refugee issue with Afghanistan.
- Boundary issues in the Rann of Kutch, Ferozepur, Pathankot and the Siachen Glacier in Kashmir with India.
- Dispute over Kori Creek and the maritime boundary with India.
- Junagarh; state that acceded to Pakistan but occupied and annexed by India; issue with India.
- Water-sharing problems with India over the Indus River (Wular Barrage)
- Illicit drugs

Pakistan is also a producer of illicit opium and hashish for the international drug trade (poppy cultivation in 1999 - 15.7 km^2, a 48% drop from 1998 because of eradication and alternative development); key transit area for Southwest Asian heroin moving to Western markets; narcotics still move from Afghanistan into Balochistan, Pakistan. (*See also: Golden Crescent and Opium production in Afghanistan*)

REFERENCES

Pakistan: The Most Allied Ally in Asia.

"Pakistan's $4.2 Billion 'Blank Check' for U.S. Military Aid, After 9/11, funding to country soars with little oversight" (in English), Center for Public Integrity (March 27, 2007).

Speech of H.E. Mr. Sergey Peskov, Ambassador Extraordinary and Plenipotentiary of the Russian Federation to the Islamic Republic of Pakistan at the Jubilee Function on the occasion of celebration of the 60th anniversary of the establishment of diplomatic relations between Russia and Pakistan - Official Website of the Embassy of the Russian Federation in the Islamic Republic of Pakistan.

5

Foreign Relations of Nepal

Nepal officially known as the Federal Democratic Republic of Nepal, is a landlocked country in South Asia and is the world's youngest republic. It is bordered to the north by the People's Republic of China, and to the south, east, and west by the Republic of India. With an area of 147,181 square kilometers and a population of approximately 30 million, Nepal is the world's 93rd largest country by land mass and the 41st most populous country. Kathmandu is the nation's capital and the country's largest metropolitan city. Nepal is a country of highly diverse and rich geography, culture, and religions. The mountainous north contains eight of the world's ten highest mountains, including the highest, Mt. Everest.

BASIC FACTS

Capital	Kathmandu
Official languages	Nepali
Recognised regional languages	Maithili, Nepal Bhasa, Bhojpuri, Tharu, Gurung, Tamang, Magar, Awadhi, Sherpa, Kiranti and other 100 different indigenous languages.
Government	Republic
– President	Ram Baran Yadav
Unification	
– Kingdom declared	December 21, 1768
– State declared	January 15, 2007

contd...

– Republic declared	May 28, 2008
Area	
– Total	147,181 km^2
– Water (%)	2.8
Population	
– July 2008 estimate	29,519,114
– 2007 census	28,875,140
GDP (PPP)	2008 estimate
– Total	$31.582 billion
– Per capita	$1,142
HDI (2007)	0.534 (medium) (142nd)
Currency	Rupee (NPR)

Nepal has traditionally maintained a non-aligned policy and enjoys friendly relations with neighboring countries, especially India and China. Constitutionally, foreign policy is to be guided by "the principles of the United Nations Charter, nonalignment, Panchsheel [five principles of peaceful coexistence], international law and the value of world peace." In practice, foreign policy has not been directed toward projecting influence internationally but toward preserving autonomy and addressing domestic economic and security issues. Nepal's most substantive international relations are perhaps with international economic institutions, such as the Asian Development Bank, the International Monetary Fund, the World Bank, and the South Asian Association for Regional Cooperation, a multilateral economic development association.

Nepal also has strong bilateral relations with major providers of economic and military aid, such as France, Germany, Japan, Switzerland, the United States, and particularly the United Kingdom, with whom military ties date to the nineteenth century. The country also maintains strong political relations with India and China, usually attempting to balance one against the other. However, relations with India are fraught with trade and border disputes and Indian suspicions that Nepalese and Pakistani rebels use Nepal as a haven to attack India. Relations with Bhutan have been strained since 1992 over the nationality and possible repatriation of refugees from Bhutan.

With People's Republic of China and India

As a small, landlocked country wedged between two larger and far stronger powers, Nepal maintains good relations with both China (People's Republic of China) and India. Because of strong cultural, religious, linguistic, and economic ties, Nepal's association with India traditionally has been close. India and Nepal restored trade relations in 1990, after a break caused by India's security concerns over Nepal's relations with the PRC. A bilateral trade treaty was signed in 1996. Nepalese can freely travel and do business in India without visa. Nepal's economy has also benefited from the surge in India's economy. Apart from Bhutan, Nepal is the only country which has open borders with India. Nepal formally established relations with the PRC in 1955, and since then their bilateral relations have generally been very good. As much as 20 thousand Tibetan refugees live in Nepal and this has been a major issue of concern between China and Nepal. Kathmandu has in several instances been brutally cracking down on the activities of the Tibetans receiving international condemnation. In 2005, Nepalese Foreign Minister Ramesh Nath Pandey called China "an all weather friend" and King Gyanendra's regime was also instrumental in inducting China into the SAARC. It received military assistance from Beijing irking India which in turn, facilitated an understanding of the underground Maoists and political parties against the King in Nov. 2005. After the success of the people's movement in April 2006, however, Sino-Nepal relations did not see any negative fall-out. Prime Minister Pushpa Kamal Dahal "Prachanda" made China his first foreign visit abroad after swearing in as the republic's first Prime Minister.

With the European Union

The European Union (EU) to Nepal relations is the relations between Nepal and the European Union (EU). The role of the European Union is to present, explain and implement EU policies, analyse and report on the political, social, and economic situation in Nepal, and to conducts negotiations in accordance with a given mandate.

With Pakistan

The bilateral relations between the Federal Democratic Republic of Nepal and the Islamic Republic of Pakistan were fully established between 1962 and 1963. Both nations have since sought to expand trade, strategic and military cooperation.

With Israel

Israel-Nepal relations, first established in 1960, are based on mutual security concerns. Bishweshwar Prasad Koirala, Prime Minister of Nepal from 1959 to 1960, had a strongly pro-Israel foreign policy. King Mahendra visited Israel in 1963 and maintained Koirala's special relationship.

With the United Kingdom

Relations between the UK and Nepal have historically been friendly and there have been close links between the Royal Families, although relations deteriorated when the King took power in 2005. A treaty of friendship was signed in 1923. The UK is highly regarded in Nepal. This is through historical ties, development assistance and long term support in the struggle for democratic peace in Nepal. Also of note is that through the recruitment of Gurkha soldiers by the British Army since the 19th century, Nepal has had links with the United Kingdom.

With Germany

Nepal also enjoys especially friendly ties with the Federal Republic of Germany, which is a major export market for Nepalese goods. Germany officially recognizes Nepal as a priority country for German development assistance and academic exchanges.

With the United States

Nepal-United States relations are bilateral relations between Nepal and the United States.

It is worth mentioning that the United States established official relations with Nepal in 1947 and opened its Kathmandu Embassy in 1959. Relations between the two countries have always been strong. U.S. policy objectives toward Nepal center on helping Nepal build a peaceful, prosperous, and democratic society.

Multilateral Relations

Nepal has played an active role in the formation of the economic development-oriented South Asian Association for Regional Cooperation (SAARC) and is the site of its secretariat. On international issues, Nepal follows a nonaligned policy and often votes with the Non-Aligned Movement in the United Nations. Nepal participates in a number of UN specialized agencies and is a member of the World Bank, International Monetary Fund, Colombo Plan, and the Asian Development Bank.

Human Rights Issues

Police forces sometimes use excessive force in quelling

violent demonstrations, or demonstrations that may upset 'friendly countries'. In addition, there have been reports of torture under detention and widespread reports of custodial abuse. In 2000, the government established the Human Rights Commission, a government-appointed commission with a mandate to investigate human rights violations.

Some restrictions continue on freedom of expression. Trafficking in women and child labour remain serious problems. Discrimination against women and lower castes is prevalent.

International Disputes & Other Issues

A joint border commission continues to work on small disputed sections of the border with India; India has instituted a stricter border regime to restrict transit of Maoist insurgents.

Illicit production of cannabis for domestic and international drug markets continues to ask as an international problem, as does rumours that the country operates as a transit point for opiates from Southeast Asia to the West. Similarly many Islamic and otehr terrorist outfits are said to be operating from Nepal.

REFERENCES

1. Abadi, Jacob. *Israel's Quest for Recognition and Acceptance in Asia: Garrison State Diplomacy*, 2004.
2. Baral, L.R., *Looking to the Future,* Anmol, New Delhi, 1996.
3. Vaidya, T.R. et al. *Nepal: International Perspective,* Anmol, New Delhi, 1997.

6

India's International Relations

India, is the biggest country in South Asia. It is the seventh-largest country by geographical area, the second-most populous country, and the most populous democracy in the world. Bounded by the Indian Ocean on the south, the Arabian Sea on the west, and the Bay of Bengal on the east, India has a coastline of 7,517 kilometers. It is bordered by Pakistan to the west; People's Republic of China (PRC), Nepal, and Bhutan to the north; and Bangladesh and Myanmar to the east. India is in the vicinity of Sri Lanka, the Maldives, and Indonesia in the Indian Ocean. Home to the Indus Valley Civilization and a region of historic trade routes and vast empires, the Indian subcontinent was identified with its commercial and cultural wealth for much of its long history. Four major world religions, Hinduism, Buddhism, Jainism and Sikhism originated there, while Zoroastrianism, Judaism, Christianity and Islam arrived in the first millennium CE and shaped the region's diverse culture by the British East India Company from the early eighteenth century and colonised by the United Kingdom from the mid-nineteenth century, India became an independent nation in 1947 after a struggle for independence that was marked by widespread nonviolent resistance.

India is a republic consisting of 28 states and seven union territories with a parliamentary system of democracy.

It has the world's twelfth largest economy at market exchange rates and the fourth largest in purchasing power. Economic reforms since 1991 have transformed it into one of the fastest growing economies; however, it still suffers from high levels of poverty, illiteracy, and malnutrition.

BASIC FACTS	
Capital	New Delhi
Official languages	Hindi, English Hindi in the Devanagari script is the official language of the Union and English the "subsidiary official language".
Constitutionally recognised languages	8th Schedule: Assamese Bengali Bodo Dogri Gujarati Hindi Kannada Kashmiri Konkani Maithili Malayalam Manipuri Marathi Nepali Oriya Punjabi Sanskrit Santali Sindhi Tamil Telugu Urdu
Government	Federal republicParliamentary democracy
– President	Pratibha Patil
– Prime Minister	Manmohan Singh
Legislature	Sansad
– Upper House	Rajya Sabha
– Lower House	Lok Sabha
Independence	from United Kingdom
– Declared	15 August 1947
– Republic	26 January 1950
Area	
– Total	3,287,240‡ km^2
– Water (%)	9.56
Population	
– 2008 estimate	1,147,995,904
– 2001 census	1,028,610,328
– Density	349/km^2 (32nd)904/sq mi
GDP (PPP)	2008 estimate
– Total	$3,288 trillion
– Per capita	$2,762
HDI (2008)	0.609 (medium)
Currency	Indian rupee

India is the world's most-populous electoral democracy and has one of the fastest economic growth rates in the world (8.9 percent GDP increase in 2007, the second-fastest growing major economy in the world after China). With the world's third largest armed forces, and fourth largest economy by purchasing power parity, it is considered to be a global power, a regional power and a middle power. It is India's growing international influence that increasingly gives it a more prominent voice in global affairs.

India has a long history of collaboration with several countries and is considered a leader of the developing world. India was one of the founding members of several international organizations, most notably the United Nations, the Non-Aligned Movement, the Asian Development Bank and the G20 industrial nations. India has also played an important and influential role in other international organizations like East Asia Summit, World Trade Organization, IMF, G8+5 and IBSA Dialogue Forum. Regional organizations India is a part of include SAARC and BIMSTEC. India has taken part in several UN peacekeeping missions and in 2007, it was the second-largest troop contributor to the United Nations. India is currently seeking a permanent seat in the UNSC, along with the G4 nations.

Even before independence, the Government of British India maintained semi-autonomous diplomatic relations. It had colonies (such as the Aden Settlement), sent and received full diplomatic missions, and was a founder member of both the League of Nations and the United Nations. After India gained independence from the United Kingdom in 1947, it soon joined the Commonwealth of Nations and strongly supported independence movements in other colonies, like the Indonesian National Revolution. The partition and various territorial disputes, particularly that over Kashmir, would strain its relations with Pakistan for years to come.

During the Cold War, India adopted a foreign policy of not aligning itself with any major power bloc. However, India developed close ties with the Soviet Union and received extensive military support from it. The end of the Cold War significantly affected India's foreign policy, as it did for much of the world. The country now seeks to strengthen its diplomatic and economic ties with the United States, the People's Republic of China, the European Union, Japan, Israel, Mexico, and Brazil. India has also forged close ties with the member states of the Association of Southeast Asian Nations, the African Union, the Arab League and Iran.

Though India continues to have a military relationship with Russia, Israel has emerged as India's second largest military partner while India has built a strong strategic partnership with the United States. The Indo-US civilian nuclear agreement, signed and implemented in 2008, highlighted the growing sophistication of the Indo-American relations similarly recent offical visit of Indian Prime Minister to USA has strengthered the relationships.

Major Elements of Policy

India's foreign policy has always regarded the concept of neighborhood as one of widening concentric circles, around a central axis of historical and cultural commonalties. The guiding principles of India's Foreign Policy have been founded on Panchsheel, pragmatism and pursuit of national interest. In a period of rapid and continuing change, foreign policy must be capable of responding optimally to new challenges and opportunities.

It has to be an integral part of the larger effort of

building the nation's capabilities through economic development, strengthening social fabric and well-being of the people and protecting India's sovereignty and territorial integrity. India's foreign policy is a forward-looking engagement with the rest of the world, based on a rigorous, realistic and contemporary assessment of the bilateral, regional and global geo-political and economic milieu.

As many as 20 million people of Indian origin live and work abroad and constitute an important link with the mother country. An important role of India's foreign policy has been to ensure their welfare and well being within the framework of the laws of the country where they live.

No exaggeration Jawaharlal Nehru set the pattern for the formation of Indian foreign policy: a strong personal role for the prime minister but a weak institutional structure. Nehru served concurrently as prime minister and minister of external affairs; he made all major foreign policy decisions himself after consulting with his advisers and then entrusted the conduct of international affairs to senior members of the Indian Foreign Service. His successors continued to exercise considerable control over India's international dealings, although they generally appointed separate ministers of external affairs.

India's second prime minister, Lal Bahadur Shastri (1964-66), expanded the Office of Prime Minister and enlarged its powers. By the 1970s, the Office of the Prime Minister had become the de facto coordinator and supraministry of the Indian government. The enhanced role of the office strengthened the prime minister's control over foreign policy making at the expense of the Ministry of External Affairs. Advisers in the office provided channels of information and policy recommendations in addition to those offered by the Ministry of External Affairs.

A subordinate part of the office—the Research and Analysis Wing (RAW)—functioned in ways that significantly expanded the information available to the prime minister and his advisers. The RAW gathered intelligence, provided intelligence analysis to the Office of the Prime Minister, and conducted covert operations abroad. The prime minister's control and reliance on personal advisers in the Office of the Prime Minister was particularly strong under the tenures of Indira Gandhi (1966-77 and 1980-84) and her son, Rajiv (1984-89), who succeeded her, and weaker during the periods of coalition governments. Observers find it difficult to determine whether the locus of decision-making authority on any particular issue lies with the Ministry of External Affairs, the Council of Ministers, the Office of the Prime Minister, or the prime minister himself. The Prime Minister is however free to appoint advisers and special committees to examine various foreign policy options and areas of interest.

In a recent instance, Manmohan Singh appointed K. Subrahmanyam in 2005 to head a special government task force to study 'Global Strategic Developments' over the next decade. The Task Force submitted its conclusions to the Prime Minister in 2006. The report has not yet been released in the public domain.

The Ministry of External Affairs (MEA) is the foreign ministry of India. It is the Indian government agency responsible for the foreign relations of India. The Minister of External Affairs holds cabinet rank as a member of the Council of Ministers.

India's relations with the world have evolved since the British Raj (1757–1947), when the British Empire monopolized external and defense relations. When India gained independence in 1947, few Indians had experience in making or conducting foreign policy. However, the country's oldest political party, the Indian National Congress, had established a small foreign department in 1925 to make overseas contacts and to publicize its freedom struggle. From the late 1920s on, Jawaharlal Nehru, who had a long-standing interest in world affairs among independence leaders, formulated the Congress stance on international issues. As a member of the interim government in 1946, Nehru articulated India's approach to the world.

During Nehru's tenure as the first Prime Minister of India (1947-64), he achieved a domestic consensus on the definition of Indian national interests and foreign policy goals — building a unified and integrated nation-state based on secular, democratic principles; defending Indian territory and protecting its security interests; guaranteeing India's independence internationally through nonalignment; and promoting national economic development unencumbered by over-reliance on any country or group of countries. These objectives were closely related to the determinants of India's foreign relations: the historical legacy of South Asia; India's geopolitical position and security requirements; and India's economic needs as a large developing nation. From 1947 until the late 1980s, India's foreign policy goals enabled it to achieve some successes in carving out an independent international role. Regionally, India was the predominant power because of its size, its population (the world's second-largest after China), and its growing military strength. However, relations with its neighbors, Pakistan in particular, were often tense and fraught with conflict. In addition, globally India's nonaligned stance was not a viable substitute for the political and economic role it wished to play. India's international influence varied over the years after independence. Indian prestige and moral authority were high in the 1950s and facilitated the acquisition of developmental assistance from both East and West. Although the prestige stemmed from India's nonaligned stance, the nation was unable to prevent Cold War politics from becoming intertwined with interstate relations in South Asia. In the 1960s and 1970s, India's international position among developed and developing countries faded in the course of wars with China and Pakistan, disputes with other countries in South Asia, and India's attempt to balance Pakistan's support from the United States and China by signing the Indo-Soviet Treaty of Friendship and Cooperation in August 1971. Although India obtained substantial Soviet military and economic aid, which helped to strengthen the nation, India's influence was undercut regionally and internationally by the perception that its friendship with the Soviet Union prevented a more forthright condemnation of the Soviet presence in Afghanistan. In the late 1980s, India improved relations with the United States, other developed countries, and China while continuing close ties with the Soviet Union. Relations with its South Asian neighbors, especially Pakistan, Sri Lanka, and Nepal, occupied much of the energies of the Ministry of External Affairs.

In the 1990s, India's economic problems and the demise of the bipolar world political system forced India to reassess its foreign policy and adjust its foreign relations. Previous policies proved inadequate to cope with the serious domestic and international problems facing India. The end of the Cold War gutted the core meaning of nonalignment and left Indian foreign policy without significant direction. The hard, pragmatic considerations of the early 1990s were still viewed within the nonaligned framework of the past, but the disintegration of the Soviet Union removed much of India's international leverage, for which relations with Russia and the other post-Soviet states could not compensate.

After the collapse of the Soviet Union, India improved its relations with the United States, Canada, France, Japan and Germany. In 1992, India established formal diplomatic relations with Israel and this relationship is growing in BJP government and progressive.

In the mid-1990s, India attracted the world attention towards the alleged Pakistan-backed terrorism in Kashmir. The Kargil War resulted in a major diplomatic victory for India. The United States and European Union recognized the fact that Pakistani military had illegally infiltrated into Indian territory and pressurized Pakistan to withdraw from Kargil. Several anti-India militant groups based in Pakistan were labeled as terrorist groups by the United States and European Union.

In 1998, India tested nuclear weapons for the second time which resulted in several U.S., Japanese and European sanctions on India. India's then defense minister, George Fernandes, said that India's nuclear program was necessary as it provided a deterrence to potential Chinese nuclear threat. Most of the sanctions imposed on India were removed by 2001.

After the September 11, 2001 attacks, Indian intelligence agencies provided the U.S. with significant information on Al-Qaeda and related groups' activities in Pakistan and Afghanistan. India's extensive contribution to the War on Terrorism, coupled with a surge in its economy, has helped India's diplomatic relations with several countries. Over the past three years, India has held numerous joint military exercises with U.S. and European nations that have resulted in a strengthened U.S.-India and E.U.-India bilateral relationship. India's bilateral trade with Europe and U.S. has more than doubled in the last five years.

India has been pushing for reforms in the UN and WTO with mixed results. India's candidature for a permanent seat at the UN Security Council is currently backed by several countries including France, Russia, the United Kingdom, Germany, Japan, Brazil Australia, African Union nations and recently China. In 2004, the United States signed a nuclear co-operation agreement with India even though the latter is not a part of the Nuclear Non-Proliferation Treaty. The US argued that India's strong nuclear non-proliferation record made it an exception, however this has not persuaded other Nuclear Suppliers Group members to sign similar deals with India.

Along these lines, in late 2008, the Indian navy sent two ships into the Gulf of Aden to protect international shipping, particularly Indian vessels, from increasing piracy off Somalia. On November 11, one of the vessels, the INS *Tabar*, was called into action to fight off a pirate attack on an Indian and a Saudi-registered vessel. In response to prompt action and successes there were calls in India to step up to the plate, much like the calls following the Indian embassy bombing in Kabul. All India Port and Dock Workers' Federation president, S R Kulkarni, suggested India take the lead ask the UN to deploy warships off the Somalia waters plagued by incessant cases of ship hijacks by pirates. He followed this call saying, "Indian warships, their officers and crew have demonstrated exemplary work by foiling hijack bid near Somalia." This was said to mark a significant step for India, which was determined to translate the said growing economic strength into global military and political clout. Ashok Mehta, a retired Indian army general, said "India now has the demonstrable capacity to project force beyond its border." He added that this was the first time commandos had been used so far from Indian shores. This follows a programme to expand the navy from having traditional coast guard duties to one of the world's largest sea forces. Indian naval chief, Adm. Sureesh Mehta, vowed that the navy would ensure "a secure and peaceful environment in the Indian Ocean region and further India's political, economic, diplomatic and military objectives." To this end, India was seeking to acquire the biggest visible symbols of naval power—aircraft carriers and nuclear submarines. In a more high-profile follow-up that got global media attention. In a more high-profile and controversial follow-up just over a week later, that had also got more global media attention, the INS *Tabar*, equipped with the guided missiles, attacked what it thought was a "mothership" of pirates, while also forcing the abandonment of another, after coming under fire. The attack continued for three-four hours. Indian naval spokesman, Commander Nirad Sinha, said that the "*INS Tabar* encountered a pirate vessel south west of Oman with two speedboats in tow. This vessel was similar in description to the 'mother vessel' mentioned in various piracy bulletins. *INS Tabar* closed in on the vessel and asked her to stop for investigation. Pirates were seen roaming on the upper deck of the vessel with guns and rocket propelled grenade launchers.

The vessel continued threatening calls and subsequently fired upon *INS Tabar*." It later turned out the sunken ship was a Thai-owned fishing vessel with 16 sailors on board. One sailor was confirmed to have survived, while another died; fourteen of the sailors' fate was not known. Since November 2 - 19, the Indian naval operations in the area had successfully escorted approximately 35 ships, including a number of non-Indian flagged vessels, safely during their transit through pirate-infested waters of the Gulf of Aden. The spokesperson signalled the need for greater multilateral coordinations when he said that "the navies of several countries...have sent their ships to protect their own shipping...We try to coordinate patrols with the other countries but it is done at an informal level."

In response to the attack it was reported that India was considering a further force augmentation to for anti-piracy operations. Even at the time of the incident the Navy was in the process of deploying a maritime reconnaissance aircraft in order to respond to merchant vessels under pirate attack more quickly. The matter was reported to be high on the agenda of defence dialogues between India and France that began just days later. Following international praise and U.N. sanction authorising India to go in "hot pursuit" of pirates vessels, India decided to bring the INS *Mysore* as it was a larger ship and better able to deal with a "growing menace." An Indian naval source said that "The UN approval which allows Indian warships to enter Somali waters has been conveyed to us recently, [and] We can now enter the Somali territorial waters under certain circumstances. It would be only to check piracy." This in turn follows Indian calls for greater cooperation in this fight against piracy.

India reached out to Pakistan as well when the country gave stern warning that it was ready to go by all means necessary to protect itself. The first step came in in an assessment that India *may* share the latest developments in its investigations into the February 2007 Samjhauta Express bombings as Pakistan was expected to reiterate that India share with them the progress in the investigation. As Pakistani president Asif Ali Zardari promised a "no first use" policy on its nuclear weapons India was set to review progress on the composite dialogue process during the Pakistani foreign minister, Shah Mehmood Qureshi visit on Wednesday. At the same time, as legislative assembly election were running in Jammu and Kashmir. The elections has triggered a war of words between India and Pakistan. The Indian ministry of external affairs has strongly objected to comments made by the Pakistan foreign ministry, questioning the credibility of the ongoing democratic process in Jammu and Kashmir and Indian External Affairs spokesperson commented on Pakistan's reaction to the election that it was "most unfortunate that Pakistan has commented on an internal matter of India. We strongly object to these remarks." The Ministry added that Pakistan ought to behave in a responsible manner as "It is in Pakistan's own interest to play a responsible role in the region. Comments such as these hardly suggest that it is prepared to do so." This came at the time when Pakistan's Indus Water Commissioner Jamaat Ali Shah said India could make Pakistan a barren land by 2014 by blocking water through construction of dams in violation of the Indus Water Treaty. He said that India had, and continued to, construct dams at various rivers in violation of the Treaty. He said that the Treaty allowed India to generate electricity on the flow of the river but it also said that water to Pakistan cannot be stopped.

Bilateral and Regional Relations

With Afghanistan

Bilateral relations between India and Afghanistan have been traditionally strong and friendly. While India was the only South Asian country to recognize the Soviet-backed Democratic Republic of Afghanistan in the 1980s, its relations were diminished during the Afghan civil wars and the rule of the Islamist Taliban in the 1990s. India aided the overthrow of the Taliban and became the largest regional provider of humanitarian and reconstruction aid. The new democratically-elected Afghan government strengthened its ties with India in wake of persisting tensions and problems with Pakistan, which was suspected of continuing to shelter and support the Taliban.

India pursues a policy of close cooperation in order to bolster its standing as a regional power and contain its rival Pakistan, which it maintains is supporting Islamic militants in Kashmir and other parts of India. India is the largest regional investor in Afghanistan, having committed more than US$2.2 billion for reconstruction purposes in the country.

With Bangladesh

Both states are part of the Indian subcontinent and have had a long common cultural, economic and political history. India played a crucial part in Bangladesh's independence from Pakistan. The people of the two countries are indistinguishable to most outsiders. The cultures of the two countries are similar; in particular India's West Bengal and Tripura states and Bangladesh are all Bengali speaking regions. India gave large amounts of aid to Bangladesh. In recent years India provides co-operation and assistance during annual natural calamities. India is a supplier of staple foods such as rice and live animals which helps keep their prices affordable for the masses of Bangladesh. Most of differences are of sharing water resources between the two countries. Also Bangladesh has been accused of providing shelter to militants.

With Bhutan

Historically, ties with India have been close. Both countries signed a Friendship treaty in 1949, where India would assist Bhutan in foreign relations. On February 8, 2007, the Indo-Bhutan Friendship Treaty was substantially revised under the Bhutanese King, Jigme Khesar Namgyel Wangchuck. Whereas in the Treaty of 1949 Article 2 read as "The Government of India undertakes to exercise no interference in the internal administration of Bhutan. On its part the Government of Bhutan agrees to be guided by the advice of the Government of India in regard to its external relations." In the revised treaty it now reads as, "In keeping with the abiding ties of close friendship and cooperation between Bhutan and India, the Government of the Kingdom of Bhutan and the Government of the Republic of India shall cooperate closely with each other on issues relating to their national interests.

Neither government shall allow the use of its territory for activities harmful to the national security and interest of the other." The revised treaty also includes in it the preamble "Reaffirming their respect for each other's independence, sovereignty and territorial integrity", an element that was absent in the earlier version. The Indo-Bhutan Friendship Treaty of 2007 strengthens Bhutan's status as an independent and sovereign nation.

With Myanmar

It is should be remembered that India was one of the leading supporters of Burmese independence and established diplomatic relations after Burma's independence from Great Britain in 1948. For many years, Indo-Burmese relations were strong due to cultural links, flourishing commerce, common interests in regional affairs and the presence of a significant Indian community in Burma. India provided considerable support when Burma struggled with regional insurgencies. However, the overthrow of the democratic government by the Military of Burma led to strains in ties.

Along with much of the world, India condemned the

suppression of democracy and Burma ordered the expulsion of the Burmese Indian community, increasing its own isolation from the world. Only China maintained close links with Burma while India supported the pro-democracy movement. However, due to geo-political concerns, India revived its relations and recognised the new name of Myanmar in 1993 overcoming strains over drug trafficking, the suppression of democracy and the rule of the military junta in Burma. Burma is situated to the south of the states of Mizoram, Manipur, Nagaland and Arunachal Pradesh in Northeast India. and the proximity of the People's Republic of China gives strategic importance to Indo-Burmese relations.

The Indo-Burmese border stretches over 1,600 miles and some insurgents in North-east India seek refuge in Myanmar. Consequently, India has been keen on increasing military cooperation with Myanmar in its counter-insurgency activities. In 2001, the Indian Army completed the construction of a major road along its border with Myanmar. India has also been building major roads, highways, ports and pipelines within Myanmar in an attempt to increase its strategic influence in the region and also to counter China's growing strides in the Indochina peninsula. Indian companies have also sought active participation in oil and natural gas exploration in Myanmar.In February 2007, India announced a plan to develop the Sittwe port, which would enable ocean access from Indian Northeastern states like Mizoram, via the Kaladan River. India is a major customer of Myanmarese oil and gas. In 2007, Indian exports to Myanmar totaled US$185 million, while its imports from Myanmar were valued at around US$810 million, comprising mostly of oil and gas. India has granted US$100 million credit to fund highway infrastructure projects in Myanmar, while US$ 57 million has been offered to upgrade Myanmarese railways.

A further US$27 million in grants has been pledged for road and rail projects. India is one of the few countries that has provided military assistance to the Myanmarese junta. However, there has been increasing pressure on India to cut some of its military supplies to Myanmar.

With Maldives

Strategically, India enjoys a considerable influence over Maldives' foreign policy and provides extensive security co-operation especially after Operation Cactus in 1988 during which India repelled Tamil mercenaries who invaded the country. As founder member in 1985 of the South Asian Association for Regional Cooperation, SAARC, which brings together Afghanistan, Bangladesh, Bhutan, India, Maldives, Nepal, Pakistan and Sri Lanka, the country plays a very active role in SAARC. The Maldives has taken the lead in calling for a South Asian Free Trade Agreement, the formulation of a Social Charter, the initiation of informal political consultations in SAARC forums, the lobbying for greater action on environmental issues, the proposal of numerous human rights measures such as the regional convention on child rights and for setting up a SAARC Human Rights Resource Centre. The Maldives is also an advocate of greater international profile for SAARC such as through formulating common positions at the UN. But the Maldives claims the Indian-administered territory of Minicoy as part of its country, that is inhabited by Muslims. India is starting the process to bring the island country into India's security grid. The move comes after the moderate Islamic nation approached New Delhi earlier this year over fears that one of its island resorts could be taken over by terrorists given its lack of military assets and surveillance capabilities.

India is also signing an agreement later this year which includes following things.

(a) India will permanently base two helicopters in the country to enhance its surveillance capabilities and ability to respond swiftly to threats. One helicopter from the Coast Guard is likely to be handed over during Antony's visit while another from the Navy will be cleared for transfer shortly.

(b) Maldives has coastal radars on only two of its 26 atolls. India will help set up radars on all 26 for seamless coverage of approaching vessels and aircraft.

(c) The coastal radar chain in Maldives will be networked with the Indian coastal radar system. India has already undertaken a project to install radars along its entire coastline. The radar chains of the two countries will be interlinked and a central control room in India's Coastal Command will get a seamless radar picture.

(d) The Indian Coast Guard (ICG) will carry out regular Dornier sorties over the island nation to look out for suspicious movements or vessels. The Southern Naval Command will overlook the inclusion of Maldives into the Indian security grid.

(e) Military teams from Maldives will visit the tri-services Andaman Nicobar Command (ANC) to observe how India manages security and surveillance of the critical island chain.

With Nepal

Relations between India and Nepal are close yet fraught with difficulties stemming from geography, economics, the problems inherent in big power-small power relations, and common ethnic and linguistic identities that overlap the two countries' borders. In 1950 New Delhi and Kathmandu initiated their intertwined relationship with the Treaty of Peace and Friendship and accompanying letters that defined security relations between the two countries, and an agreement governing both bilateral trade and trade transiting Indian soil. The 1950 treaty and letters stated that "neither government shall tolerate any threat to the security of the other by a foreign aggressor" and obligated both sides "to inform each other of any serious friction or misunderstanding with any neighboring state likely to cause any breach in the friendly relations subsisting between the two governments." These accords cemented a "special relationship" between India and Nepal that granted Nepal preferential economic treatment and provided Nepalese in India the same economic and educational opportunities as Indian citizens.

With Pakistan

It is remarkable that despite historical and cultural links, relations between India and Pakistan have been plagued by years of mistrust and suspicion ever since the partition of India in 1947. The principal source of contention between India and its western neighbour has been the Kashmir conflict. After an invasion by Pashtun tribesmen and Pakistani paramilitary forces, the Maharaja of the Dogra Kingdom of Jammu and Kashmir, Hari Singh, and its Prime Minister, Sheikh Abdullah, signed an Instrument of Accession with New Delhi making the state an integral part of the Union of India. The First Kashmir War started after the Indian Army entered Srinagar, the capital of the state, to secure the area from the invading forces. The war ended in December 1948 with the Line of Control dividing the erstwhile princely state into territories administered by

Pakistan (northern and western areas) and India (southern, central and northeastern areas).

Pakistan contested the legality of the Instrument of Accession since the Dogra Kingdom has signed a standstill agreement with it. The Indo-Pakistani War of 1965 started following the failure of Pakistan's Operation Gibraltar, which was designed to infiltrate forces into Jammu and Kashmir to precipitate an insurgency against rule by India. The five-week war caused thousands of casualties on both sides. It ended in a United Nations (UN) mandated ceasefire and the subsequent issuance of the Tashkent Declaration. India and Pakistan went to war again in 1971, however this time the conflict was over East Pakistan rather than Kashmir. Due to the large-scale atrocities committed by the Pakistan army, millions of Bengali refugees poured over into India. India, along with Mukti Bahini, defeated Pakistan and the Pakistani forces surrendered on the eastern front. The war resulted in the creation of Bangladesh.

In 1998, India carried out the Pokhran-II nuclear tests which was followed by Pakistan's Chagai-I tests. Following the Lahore Declaration in February 1999, relations briefly improved. However, few months later, Kashmiri insurgents and Pakistani paramilitary forces, backed by Pakistani Army, infiltrated in large numbers into the Kargil district of Indian Kashmir. This initiated the Kargil conflict after India moved in thousands of troops to successfully flush out the infiltrators. Though the conflict did not result in a full-scale war between India and Pakistan, relations between the two reached all-time low which worsened even further following Pakistan's alleged involvement in the hijacking of the Indian Airlines IC814 plane in December 1999. Attempts to normalize relations, such as the Agra summit held in July 2001, failed. Following the attack on the

Indian Parliament in December 2001, which was blamed on Pakistan, a country which had condemned the attack. There was a military standoff between the two countries which lasted for nearly a year raising fears of a nuclear conflict. However, a peace process, initiated in 2003, led to improved relations in the following years.

Since the initiation of peace process, several confidence-building-measures (CBMs) between India and Pakistan have taken shape. The Samjhauta Express and Delhi–Lahore Bus service are one of these successful measures which have played a crucial role in expanding people to people contact between the two countries. The initiation of Srinagar–Muzaffarabad Bus service in 2005 and opening of a historic trade route across the Line of Control in 2008 further reflects increasing eagerness among the two sides to improve relations. Though bilateral trade between India and Pakistan was a modest US$1.7 billion in March 2007, it is expected to cross US$10 billion by 2010.

The recent terror attacks in Mumbai, however, have seriously undermined the relations between the two countries. India is alleging Pakistan of harboring militants on their soil, while Pakistan vehemently denies such claims. The Pakistani Prime Minister Yousuf Raza Gilani, President Asif Zardari, Foreign Minister Shah Mehmood Qureshi and the Pakistani consulate in India have been at the fore-front of these denials. Relations are currently hampered since India has sent a list of 40 alleged fugitive in various terror strikes to Pakistan, expecting the handover of the said 40 people to the Indian Government. Pakistan, on the other hand, has openly declared to be having no intentions whatsoever of doing the above said extradition.

With Sri Lanka

India-Sri Lanka relations have undergone a qualitative

and quantitative transformation in the recent past. Political relations are close, trade and investments have increased dramatically, infrastructural linkages are constantly being augmented, defence collaboration has increased and there is a general, broad-based improvement across all sectors of bilateral cooperation. India was the first country to respond to Sri Lanka's request for assistance after the tsunami in December 2004. In July 2006, India evacuated 430 Sri Lankan nationals from Lebanon, first to Cyprus by Indian Navy ships and then to Delhi & Colombo by special Air India flights. There exists a broad consensus within the Sri Lankan polity on the primacy of India in Sri Lanka's external relations matrix. Both the major political parties in Sri Lanka, viz., the Sri Lanka Freedom Party and the United Nationalist Party have contributed to the rapid development of bilateral relations in the last ten years.

Australia

The strongest ties between these two states is the commonwealth connection. Cricketing and Bollywood ties also help foster relations as in the frequent travel for games, and, more importantly, the presence of Australian cricketers in India for commercial gain. This was further enhanced with the IPL, and, to a lesser degree, the ICL. Bollywood has also improved ties as with John Howard's visit to Mumbai to increase tourism to Australia. Furthermore, there is a going strategic connection to forming an "Asian NATO" with India, Japan, the US and Australia. The bilateral agreements have worked out for all but the Indo-Australian angle, though this has been hurt by India's refusal to sign the NPT and Australia's consequent refusal to provide India with uranium until the latter do so. The Australian and Indian militaries have already worked well together. Of late the relations between the two countries were jolted, with attacks on Indian Community students in Melbourne, Australia. Indian Government lodged strong protests with the Australian Government.

Australian Prime Minister Mr. Kevin Rudd said that "Australia valued its education system and International Students are valued more here in Australia." Mr. Rudd though said that his Govt. has ordered a thorough probe into the attacks and also condemned it in strongest possible terms no significant break through has been achieved.

China

Despite lingering suspicions remaining from the 1962 Sino-Indian War and continuing boundary disputes over Aksai Chin and Arunachal Pradesh, Sino-Indian relations have improved gradually since 1988. Both countries have sought to reduce tensions along the frontier, expand trade and cultural ties, and normalize relations. A series of high-level visits between the two nations have helped improve relations. In December 1996, PRC President Jiang Zemin visited India during a tour of South Asia. While in New Delhi, he signed with the Indian Prime Minister a series of confidence-building measures for the disputed borders.

Sino-Indian relations suffered a brief setback in May 1998 when the Indian Defence minister justified the country's nuclear tests by citing potential threats from the PRC. However, in June 1999, during the Kargil crisis, then-External Affairs Minister Jaswant Singh visited Beijing and stated that India did not consider China a threat. By 2001, relations between India and the PRC were on the mend, and the two sides handled the move from Tibet to India of the 17th Karmapa in January 2000 with delicacy and tact. In 2003, India formally recognized Tibet as a part of China, and China recognized Sikkim as a formal part of

India in 2004. Since 2004, the economic rise of both China and India has also helped forge closer relations between the two. Sino-Indian trade reached US$36 billion in 2007, making China the single largest trading partner of India. The increasing economic reliance between India and China has also bought the two nations closer politically, with both India and China eager to resolve their boundary dispute. They have also collaborated on several issues ranging from WTO's Doha round in 2008 to regional free trade agreement. Similar to Indo-US nuclear deal, India and China have also agreed to cooperate in the field of civilian nuclear energy. However, China's economic interests have clashed with those of India. Both the countries are the largest Asian investors in Africa and have competed for control over its large natural resources.

Fiji

Fijis relationship with the Republic of India is often seen by observers against the backdrop of the sometimes tense relations between its indigenous people and the 44 percent of the population who are of Indian descent. India has used its influence in international forums such as the Commonwealth of Nations and United Nations on behalf of ethnic Indians in Fiji, lobbying for sanctions against Fiji in the wake of the 1987 coups and the 2000 coup, both of which removed governments, one dominated and one led, by Indo-Fijians.

Japan

India-Japan relations have always been strong. India has culturally influenced Japan through Buddhism. During the Indian Independence Movement, the Japanese Imperial Army helped Netaji Subhash Chandra Bose's Indian National Army. Relations have remained warm since India's independence. Japanese companies, like Sony, Toyota, and

Honda, have manufacturing facilities in India, and with the growth of the Indian economy, India is a big market for Japanese firms. The most prominent Japanese company to have a big investment in India is automobiles giant Suzuki which is in partnership with Indian automobiles company Maruti Suzuki, the largest car manufacturer in India. In December 2006, Prime Minister Manmohan Singh's visit to Japan culminated in the signing of the "Joint Statement Towards Japan-India Strategic and Global Partnership". Japan has funded some major infrastructure projects in India, most notably the Delhi Metro subway system. Indian applicants were welcomed in 2006 to the JET Program, starting with just one slot available in 2006 and 41 in 2007. Also, in the year 2007, the Japanese Self Defence Forces took part in a naval exercise in the Indian Ocean, known as Malabar 2007, which also involved the naval forces of India, Australia, Singapore and the United States.

In October 2008, Japan signed an agreement with India under which it would grant the latter a low-interest loan worth US$4.5 billion to construct a railway project between Delhi and Mumbai. This is the single largest overseas project being financed by Japan and reflects growing economic partnership between the two. India is also one of three countries with whom Japan has security pact, the other being Australia and the United States.

Laos

In recent years, India has endeavoured to build relations, with this small Southeast Asian nation. They have strong military relations, and India shall be building an Airforce Academy in Laos.

Indonesia

In 1950, the first President of Indonesia - Sukarno

called upon the peoples of Indonesia and India to "intensify the cordial relations" that had existed between the two countries "for more than 1000 years" before they had been "disrupted" by colonial powers. Fifteen years later in Djakarta, government-inspired mobs were shouting: "Down with India, the servant of imperialists" and "Crush India, our enemy. " Yet in the spring of 1966, the foreign ministers of both countries began speaking again of an era of friendly relations. India had supported Indonesian independence and Nehru had raised the Indonesian question in the United Nations Security Council. Today, India has an embassy in Jakarta and Indonesia operates an embassy in Delhi.

Malaysia

India has a high commission in Kuala Lumpur, and Malaysia has a high commission in New Delhi. Both countries are full members of the Commonwealth of Nations, and the Asian Union. India and Malaysia are also connected by various cultural and historical ties that date back to antiquity. The two countries are on excellently friendly terms with each other seeing as Malaysia is home to a strong concentration of Indian immigrants.

Singapore

India and Singapore share long-standing cultural, commercial and strategic relations, with Singapore being a part of the "Greater India" cultural and commercial region. More than 300,000 people of Indian origin live in Singapore. Following its independence in 1965, Singapore was concerned with China-backed communist threats as well as domination from Malaysia and Indonesia and sought a close strategic relationship with India, which it saw as a counter-balance to Chinese influence and a partner in achieving regional security. Singapore had always been an important strategic trading post, giving India trade access to Maritime Southeast Asia and the Far East. Although the rival positions of both nations over the Vietnam War and the Cold War caused consternation between India and Singapore, their relationship expanded significantly in the 1990s; Singapore was one of the first to respond to India's "Look East" Policy of expanding its economic, cultural and strategic ties in Southeast Asia to strengthen its standing as a regional power. Singapore, and especially, the Singaporean Foreign Minister, George Yeo, have taken an interest, in re-establishing the ancient Indian university, Nalanda University.

Singapore is the 8th largest source of investment in India and the largest amongst ASEAN member nations. It is also India's 9th biggest trading partner as of 2005-06. Its cumulative investment in India totals USD 3 billion as of 2006 and is expected to rise to US 5 billion by 2010 and US 10 billion by 2015. India's economic liberalisation and its "Look East" policy have led to a major expansion in bilateral trade, which grew from USD 2.2 billion in 2001 to US 9-10 billion in 2006 - a 400% growth in span of five years - and to USD 50 billion by 2010. Singapore accounts for 38% of India's trade with ASEAN member nations and 3.4% of its total foreign trade. India's main exports to Singapore in 2005 included petroleum, gemstones, jewellery, machinery and its imports from Singapore included electronic goods, organic chemicals and metals. More than half of Singapore's exports to India are basically "re-exports" - items that had been imported from India.

South Korea

The cordial relationship between the two countries extends back to 48AD, when Queen Suro, or Princess Heo, travelled from the kingdom of Ayodhya to Korea. According to the Samguk Yusa, the princess had a dream about a heavenly king who was awaiting heaven's anointed ride. After Princess Heo had the dream, she asked her parents, the king and queen, for permission to set out and seek the man, which the king and queen urged with the belief that god orchestrated the whole fate. Upon approval, she set out on a boat, carrying gold, silver, a tea plant, and a stone which calmed the waters. Archeologists discovered a stone with two fish kissing each other, a symbol of the Gaya kingdom that is unique to the Mishra royal family in Ayodhya, India. This royal link provides further evidence that there was an active commercial engagements between India and Korea since the queen's arrival to Korea. Current descendants live in the city of Kimhae as well as abroad in America's state of New Jersey and Kentucky. Many of them became prominent and well-known around the world like President Kim Dae Jung, Prime Minister Jong Pil Kim. The relations between the countries have been relatively limited, although much progress arose during the three decades. Since the formal establishment of the diplomatic ties between two countries in 1973, several trade agreements have been reached. Trade between the two nations has increased exponentially, exemplified by the $530 million during the fiscal year of 1992–1993, and the $10 billion during 2006–2007. During the 1997 Asian financial crisis, South Korean businesses sought to increase access to the global markets, and began trade investments with India. The last two presidential visits from South Korea to India were in 1996 and 2006, and the embassy works between the two countries are seen as needing improvements. Recently, there have been acknowledgements in the Korean public and political spheres that expanding relations with India should be a major economical and political priority for South Korea. Much of the economic investments of

South Korea have been drained into China; however, South Korea is currently the fifth largest source of investment in India. To the Times of India, President Roh voiced his opinion that cooperation between India's software and Korea's IT industries would bring very efficient and successful outcomes. The two countries agreed to shift their focus to the revision of the visa policies between the two countries, expansion of trade, and establishment of free trade agreement to encourage further investment between the two countries.

Korean companies such as LG and Samsung have established manufacturing and service facilities in India, and several Korean construction companies won grants for a portion of the many infrastructural building plans in India, such as the "National Highway Development Project".

Taiwan

The bilateral relations between India and Taiwan (officially *Republic of China*) have improved since the 1990s despite both nations *not* maintaining official diplomatic relations, India recognizes only the People's Republic of China and not the Republic of China's contention of being the legitimate government of territorial China - a conflict that emerged after the Chinese Civil War (1945-49). However, India's economic & Commercial links as well as people-to-people contacts with Taiwan have expanded in recent years.

Thailand

India's Look East policy, saw India grow relations with ASEAN countries including Thailand, and Thailand's Look West policy, also saw it grow its relations with India. Both countries are members of BIMSTEC. Indian Prime Ministers Rajiv Gandhi, P.V. Narasimha Rao, Atal Bihari Vajpayee, and Manmohan Singh, have visited Thailand as have, Chatichai Choonhavan, Thaksin Shinawatra, and Surayud Chulanont, visited India. In 2003, a Free trade agreement was signed between the two countries. India, is the 13th largest investor in Thailand. The spheres of trade are in chemicals, pharmaceuticals, textiles, nylon, tyre cord, real estate, rayon fibres, paper grade pulps, steel wires, and rods. However, IT Services, and manufacturing, are the main spheres. Through Buddhism, India, has culturally influenced Thailand. The Indian epics, Mahabharata, and Ramayana, are popular and are widely taught in schools as part of the curriculum in Thailand. The example can also be seen in temples around Thailand, where the story of Ramayana and renowned Indian folk stories are depicted on the temple wall Thailand, has become a big tourist destination for Indians.

Vietnam

India supported Vietnam's independence from France, opposed U.S. involvement in the Vietnam War and supported unification of Vietnam. India established official diplomatic relations in 1972 and maintained friendly relations, especially in wake of Vietnam's hostile relations with the People's Republic of China, which had become India's strategic rival. India granted the "Most Favoured Nation" status to Vietnam in 1975 and both nations signed a bilateral trade agreement in 1978 and the Bilateral Investment Promotion and Protection Agreement (BIPPA) on March 8, 1997.

In 2007, a fresh joint declaration was issued during the state visit of the Prime Minister of Vietnam Nguyen Tan Dung. Bilateral trade has increased rapidly since the liberalisation of the economies of both Vietnam and India. India is the 13th-largest exporter to Vietnam, with exports have grown steadily from USD 11.5 million in 1985-86 to

USD 395.68 million by 2003. Vietnam's exports to India rose to USD 180 million, including agricultural products, handicrafts, textiles, electronics and other goods. Between 2001 and 2006, the volume of bilateral trade expanded at 20-30% per annum to reach USD 1 billion by 2006. Continuing the rapid pace of growth, bilateral trade is expected to rise to USD 2 billion by 2008, 2 years ahead of the official target. India and Vietnam have also expanded cooperation in information technology, education and collaboration of the respective national space programmes.

Direct air links and lax visa regulations have been established to bolster tourism. India and Vietnam are members of the Mekong-Ganga Cooperation, created to develop to enhance close ties between India and nations of Southeast Asia. Vietnam has supported India's bid to become a permanent member of the U.N. Security Council and join the Asia-Pacific Economic Cooperation (APEC). In the 2003 joint declaration, India and Vietnam envisaged creating an "Arc of Advantage and Prosperity" in Southeast Asia; to this end, Vietnam has backed a more important relationship and role between India and the Association of Southeast Asian Nations (ASEAN) and its negotiation of an Indo-ASEAN free trade agreement.

India and Vietnam have also built strategic partnerships, including extensive cooperation on developing nuclear power, enhancing regional security and fighting terrorism, transnational crime and drug trafficking.

Argentina

(a) Formal relations started on 1949-02-03

(b) India has an embassy in Buenos Aires.

(c) Argentina has an embassy in New Delhi.

(d) Indians have expressed its desires to agree with

the Argentinian claims on British colonies in Southern Atlantic Ocean and other territorial border disputes with Chile.

(e) List of Treaties ruling relations Argentina and India (Argentine Foreign Ministry, in Spanish)

(f) Indian embassy in Buenos Aires

Brazil

Brazil and India are large continental sized countries with social diversity, democratic governments, a multiethnic society, and a large population base. Both possess advanced technologies. The two countries share similar perceptions on issues of interest to developing countries and have cooperated in the multilateral level on issues such as international trade and development, environment, reform of the UN and the UNSC expansion.There is enormous interest in Brazil on India's culture, religion, performing arts and philosophy. Mohandas Gandhi is highly regarded in the country and the government has sought to teach his philosophy of non-violence to the police to improve its track record. A statue of Mahatma Gandhi is located in a prominent square in Rio de Janeiro.

A group called the Filhos de Gandhi (Sons of Gandhi) participates regularly in the carnival in Salvador. Private Brazilian organizations occasionally invite Indian cultural troupes. In recent years, relations between Brazil and India have grown considerably and co-operation between the two countries has been extended to such diverse areas as science and technology, pharmaceuticals and space. The two-way trade in 2007 nearly tripled to US$ 3.12 billion from US$ 1.2 billion in 2004.

India attaches tremendous importance to its relationship with this Latin American giant and hopes to see the areas of co-operation expand in the coming years. Both countries want the participation of developing countries in the UNSC permanent membership since the underlying philosophy for both of them are: UNSC should be more democratic, legitimate and representative - the G4 is a novel grouping for this realization. Brazil and India are deeply committed to IBSA (South-South cooperation) initiatives and attach utmost importance to this trilateral cooperation between the three large, multi-ethnic, multi-racial and multi-religious developing countries, which are bound by the common principle of pluralism and democracy.

Canada

Indo-Canadian relations, are the longstanding bilateral relations between India and Canada, which are built upon a "mutual commitment to democracy", "pluralism", and "people-to-people links," according to the government of Canada. In 2004, bilateral trade between India and Canada was at about C$2.45 billion. However, the botched handling of the Air India investigation and the case in general suffered a setback to Indo-Canadian relations. India's Smiling Buddha nuclear test led to connections between the two countries being frozen, with allegations that India broke the terms of the Colombo Plan. Although Jean Chrétien and Roméo LeBlanc both visited India in the late 1990s, relations were again halted after the Pokhran-II tests.

Colombia

Both countries established diplomatic ties on January 19, 1959. Since then the relationship between the two countries has been gradually increasing with more frequent diplomatic visits to promote political, commercial cultural and academic exchanges. Colombia is currently the commercial point of entry into Latin America for Indian companies.

Mexico

Mexico is a very important and major economic partner of India. Mexico and India, both have embassies in the other country. Octavio Paz worked as a diplomat in India. His book *In Light of India* is an analysis of Indian history and culture.

Paraguay

India and Paraguay established diplomatic relations on September 13, 1961. India is represented in Paraguay through its embassy in Buenos Aires, Argentina and an honorary consulate in Asuncion. Since 2005, Paraguay has had an embassy in New Delhi.

United States of America

Historically, relations between India and the United States were somewhat cold following Indian independence, as India took a leading position in the Non-Aligned Movement, and attempted to pursue even-handed economic and military relations with the Soviet Union, although US provided support to India in 1962 during its war with China. For most of the Cold War, the USA tended to have warmer relations with Pakistan, primarily as a way to contain Soviet-friendly India and to use Pakistan to back the Afghan Mujahideen against the Soviet occupation of Afghanistan. An Indo-Soviet twenty year friendship treaty, signed in 1971, also positioned India against the USA. India played a key role in establishing the Non-Aligned Movement in 1961. Though India pursued close relations with both USA and USSR, it decided not to join any major power bloc and refrained from joining military alliances. India, however began establishing close military relationship with the Soviet Union. After the Sino-Indian War and the Indo-Pakistani War of 1965, India made considerable changes to its foreign policy. It developed a close relationship with the Soviet Union and started receiving massive military equipment and financial assistance from the USSR.

This had an adverse effect on the Indo-USA relationship. The United States saw Pakistan as a counter-weight to pro-Soviet India and started giving the former military assistance. This created an atmosphere of suspicion between India and USA. The USA-India relationship suffered a considerable setback during the Soviet invasion of Afghanistan when India openly supported the Soviet Union. Relations between India and the United States came to an all-time low during the early 1970s. Despite reports of atrocities in East Pakistan, and being told, most notably in the *Blood telegram*, of genocidal activities being perpetrated by Pakistani forces, U.S. Secretary of State Henry Kissinger and U.S. President Richard Nixon did nothing to discourage then Pakistani President Yahya Khan and the Pakistan Army. Kissinger was particularly concerned about Soviet expansion into South Asia as a result of a treaty of friendship that had recently been signed between India and the Soviet Union, and sought to demonstrate to the People's Republic of China the value of a tacit alliance with the United States.

During the Indo-Pakistani War of 1971, Indian Armed Forces, along with the Mukti Bahini, succeeded in liberating East Pakistan which soon declared independence. Richard Nixon, then USA President, feared that an Indian invasion of West Pakistan would mean total Soviet domination of the region, and that it would seriously undermine the global position of the United States and the regional position of America's new tacit ally, China. In order to demonstrate to China the *bona fides* of the United States as an ally, and in direct violation of the USA Congress-imposed sanctions on Pakistan, Nixon sent military supplies to Pakistan, routing them through Jordan and Iran, while also encouraging China to increase its arms supplies to Pakistan. When Pakistan's defeat in the eastern sector seemed certain, Nixon sent the USS *Enterprise* to the Bay of Bengal, a move deemed by the Indians as a nuclear threat. The *Enterprise* arrived on station on December 11, 1971. On 6 December and 13 December, the Soviet Navy dispatched two groups of ships, armed with nuclear missiles, from Vladivostok; they trailed U.S. Task Force 74 into the Indian Ocean from 18 December 1971 until 7 January 1972.

The Soviets also sent a nuclear submarine to ward off the threat posed by USS *Enterprise* in the Indian Ocean. Though American efforts had no effect in turning the tide of the war, the incident involving USS *Enterprise* is viewed as the trigger for India's subsequent nuclear program. American policy towards the end of the war was dictated primarily by a need to restrict the escalation of war on the western sector to prevent the 'dismemberment' of West Pakistan.

Years after the war, many American writers criticized the White House policies during the war as being badly flawed and ill-serving the interests of the United States. India carried out nuclear tests a few years later resulting in sanctions being imposed by United States, further drifting the two countries apart.

Since the end of the Cold War, India-USA relations have improved dramatically. This has largely been fostered by the fact that the USA and India are both democracies and have a large and growing trade relationship. During the Gulf War, the economy of India went through an extremely difficult phase. The Government of India liberalized the Indian economy.

After the break up of the Soviet Union, India started looking for new allies and tried improving diplomatic relations with the members of the NATO particularly the United States, Canada, France and Germany. In 1992, India established formal diplomatic relations with Israel. In the mid-1990s, India tried to attract world attention towards the Pakistan backed terrorism in Kashmir. The Kargil War resulted in a major diplomatic victory for India. The United States and European Union recognized the fact that Pakistani military had illegally infiltrated into Indian territory and pressured Pakistan to withdraw from Kargil. Several anti-India terrorist groups based in Pakistan were labeled as terrorist groups by the United States and European Union.

In 1998, India tested nuclear weapons which resulted in several U.S., Japanese and European sanctions on India. India's then defence minister, George Fernandes, said that India's nuclear program was necessary as it provided a deterrence to some potential nuclear threat. Most of the sanctions imposed on India were removed by 2001. India has categorically stated that it will never use weapons first but will defend if attacked.

In fact Pakistan is the first country that India informs if any nuclear tests are on the agenda. The economic sanctions imposed by the United States in response to India's nuclear tests in May 1998 appeared, at least initially, to seriously damage Indo-American relations. President Bill Clinton imposed wide-ranging sanctions pursuant to the 1994 Nuclear Proliferation Prevention Act. U.S. sanctions on Indian entities involved in the nuclear industry and opposition to international financial institution loans for non-humanitarian assistance projects in India. The United States encouraged India to sign the Comprehensive Test Ban Treaty (CTBT) immediately and without condition.

The U.S. also called for restraint in missile and nuclear testing and deployment by both India and Pakistan. The non-proliferation dialogue initiated after the 1998 nuclear tests has bridged many of the gaps in understanding between the countries.

After the September 11, 2001 attacks, Indian intelligence agencies provided the U.S. with significant information on Al-Qaeda and related groups' activities in Pakistan and Afghanistan. India's extensive contribution to the War on Terrorism has helped India's diplomatic relations with several countries. Over the past few years, India has held numerous joint military exercises with U.S. and European nations that have resulted in a strengthened U.S.-India and E.U.-India bilateral relationship. India's bilateral trade with Europe and U.S. has more than doubled in the last five years. However, India has not signed the CTBT, or the Nuclear Non-Proliferation Treaty, claiming the discriminatory nature of the treaty that allows the five declared nuclear countries of the world to keep their nuclear arsenal and develop it using computer simulation testing. Prior to its nuclear testing, India had pressed for a comprehensive destruction of nuclear weapons by all countries of the world in a time-bound frame. This was not acceptable to the USA and other countries. Presently, India has declared its policy of "no-first use of nuclear weapons" and the maintenance of a "credible nuclear deterrence". The USA, under President George W. Bush has also lifted most of its sanctions on India and has resumed military co-operation. Relations with USA have considerably improved in the recent years, with the two countries taking part in joint naval exercises off the coast of India and joint air exercises both in India as well as in the United States. India has been pushing for reforms in the UN and WTO with mixed results. India's candidature for a permanent seat at the UN Security Council is currently backed by several countries including United Kingdom, France, Germany, Japan, Brazil, African Union nations and recently People's Republic of China. In 2005, the United States signed a nuclear co-operation agreement with India even though the latter is not a part of the NPT. The US argued that India's strong nuclear non-proliferation record made it an exception and persuaded other NSG members to sign similar deals with India. On March 2, 2006 India and the USA signed the Indo-U.S. Nuclear Pact on co-operation in civilian nuclear field. This was signed during the four days state visit of USA President George Bush in India. On its part, India would separate its civilian and military nuclear programs, and the civilian programs would be brought under the safeguards of International Atomic Energy Agency (IAEA).

The United States would sell India the reactor technologies and the nuclear fuel for setting up and upgrading its civilian nuclear program. The U.S. Congress needs to ratify this pact since U.S. federal law prohibits the trading of nuclear technologies and materials outside the framework of the Nuclear Suppliers Group (NSG).

Indo-USA Strategic Partnership

Indo-USA relations got strategic content way back in early sixties. The rise of China worried the policymakers in Washington. Chinese annexation of Tibet, its role in Korean war and other such acts convinced Washington about the expansionist designs of the Chinese. As the relations between India and China deteriorated during late fifties, the Americans found a golden opportunity to take advantage of this situation to promote India as a counterweight to China. But any unidimensional alliance is bound to be short-lived and this alliance was no exception to this general rule. As China ceased to be a headache for the American policymakers by the late sixties, this unidimensional alliance disappeared into thin air.

The end of the Cold War necessitated as well as facilitated the infusion of strategic content to Indo-USA relations–this time multidimensional. In the post Cold War era, the strategic objectives of India and the USA converges on a number of issues and not just one–as well as the case earlier. These issues include, inter alia, containment of terrorism, promotion of democracy, counter proliferation, freedom of navigation in the Indian Ocean, Asian balance of power, etc.

One of the very interesting feature of Indo-USA relations of recent times is the changes on the terms of engagement between the two countries on the issue of nuclear proliferation. While earlier, in the USA strategic thinking on nuclear proliferation, India figured mainly because of American concern about latter's nuclear and missile programmes, in the twenty-first century, however, American strategic thinking on the issue of nuclear proliferation has undergone radical reorientation. Now, the Americans are increasingly realising the futility of insisting on a rollback of India's nuclear programme. They, rather, want to leverage India's growing power and influence in favour of their broader nonproliferation and counter proliferation objectives.

As promotion of democracy around the world is one of the most important foreign policy objective of the USA, India - as the largest democracy of the world-can hardly be ignored by the USA. This is the reason, cooperation in promotion of democracy in the world has become one of the most important facets of Indo-USA relations in recent times. India is a founding member of the 'Community of Democracies'

– a prominent endeavour of the USA on promotion of democracy. However, India rejected the suggestion of the USA about setting up a Centre for Asian Democracy.

Agriculture is another important area of cooperation between India and the USA in present times. Considering the fact that both the nations at present have a vast pool of human resources adept at knowledge economy, it is only natural that the most optimal course such partnership can aim at is harnessing these human resources by concentrating on development and dissemination of agricultural knowledge through research, education and training etc. An initiative to forge such a partnership is the 'India-USA Knowledge Initiative on Agriculture' (KIA).

Indian Prime Minister Manmohan Singh was the guest of honor at the first state dinner, which took place on November 24 2009, of the administration of US President Barack Obama.

European Union

India was one of the first countries to develop relations with the Union, signing bilateral agreements in 1973, when the United Kingdom joined. The most recent cooperation agreement was signed in 1994 and an action plan was signed in 2005. As of April 2007 the Commission is pursuing a free trade agreement with India.

The Union is India's largest trading partner, accounting for 20% of Indian trade. However, India accounts for only 1.8% of the EU's trade and attracts only 0.3% of European Foreign Direct Investment, although still provides India's largest source. During 2005 EU-India trade grew by 20.3%.

There was controversy in 2006 when the Indian Mittal Steel Company sought to take-over the Luxembourg based steel company, Arcelor. The approach met with opposition from France and Luxembourg but was passed by the Commission who stated that were judging it on competition grounds only.

The European Union (EU) and India agreed on September 29, 2008 at the EU-India summit in Marseille, France's largest commercial port, to expand their cooperation in the fields of nuclear energy and environmental protection and deepen their strategic partnership. French President Nicolas Sarkozy, the EU's rotating president, said at a joint press conference at the summit that "EU welcomes India, as a large country, to engage in developing nuclear energy, adding that this clean energy will be helpful for the world to deal with the global climate change." Sarkozy also said the EU and Indian Prime Minister Manmohan pledged to accelerate talks on a free trade deal and expected to finish the deal by 2009. The Indian prime minister was also cautiously optimistic about cooperation on nuclear energy. "Tomorrow we have a bilateral summit with France. This matter will come up and I hope some good results will emerge out of that meeting," Singh said when asked about the issue. Singh said that he was "very satisfied" with the results of the summit. He added that EU and India have "common values" and the two economies are complementary to each other. European Commission President Jose Manuel Barroso, also speaking at Monday's press conference, expounded the joint action plan on adjustments of EU's strategic partnership with India, saying the two sides will strengthen cooperation on world peace and safety, sustainable development, cooperation in science and technology and cultural exchanges. Reviewing the two sides' efforts in developing the bilateral strategic partnership, the joint action plan reckoned that in politics, dialogue and cooperation have enhanced through regular summits and exchanges of visits and that in economy, mutual investments have increased dramatically in recent years, dialogue in macro economic policies and financial services has established and cooperation in energy, science and technology and environment has been launched. Under the joint action plan.

EU and Indian would enhance consultation and dialogue on human rights within the UN framework, strengthen cooperation in world peacekeeping mission, fight against terror and non-proliferation of arms, promote cooperation and exchange in developing civil nuclear energy and strike a free trade deal as soon as possible. France, which relies heavily on nuclear power and is a major exporter of nuclear technology, is expected to sign a deal that would allow it to provide nuclear fuel to India. Trade between India and the 27-nation EU has more than doubled from 25.6 billion euros ($36.7 billion) in 2000 to 55.6 billion euros last year, with further expansion to be seen. "We have agreed to achieve an annual bilateral trade turnover of 100 billion euros within the next five years," Singh told reporters.

United Kingdom

Since 1947, India's relations with the United Kingdom have been through bilateral, as well as through the Commonwealth of Nations framework. Although the Sterling Area no longer exists and the Commonwealth is much more an informal forum, India and the UK still have many enduring links. This is in part due to the significant number of people of Indian origin living in the UK. The large South Asian population in the UK results in steady travel and communication between the two countries.

The British Raj allowed for both cultures to imbibe tremendously from the other. The English language and cricket are perhaps the two most evident British exports, whilst in the UK Indian music and food are fixtures in daily life. It is also notable that there are many words of Indian origin now common to the language. The United Kingdom's favourite food is reported to be Indian Cuisine, although no official study reports this. Economically the relationship between Britain and India is also strong. India is the second largest investor in Britain after the US. Britain is also one of the largest investors in India. Recently, many British jobs have been moving to the call centres in India. The Queen's visits to India have been enormously successful along with those by other members of the Royal Family. Britain has also supported India's rise to prominence on the international stage, including advocating a permanent seat on the Security Council. The UK recently gave India a £825 million aid package to help India develop its health and education systems.

France

France and India established diplomatic relationships soon after India achieved independence in 1947. India's strong diplomatic ties with France resulted in the peaceful cession of Pondicherry to India on November 1, 1954 without any military opposition from France.

France and Russia were the only countries that did not condemn India's decision to go nuclear in 1998. In 2003, France became the largest supplier of nuclear fuel and technology to India and remains a large military and economic trade partner. India's permanent member aspirations in the UN Security Council have found very strong support from former French President Chirac and more recently by the current French President Nicolas Sarkozy. The recent decision by the Indian government to purchase French Scorpène class submarines worth 3 billion USD and 43 Airbus aircraft for Air India worth 2.5 billion USD has further cemented the strategic, military and economic co-operation between India and France.

Nicolas Sarkozy visited India in January 2008 and was the Chief Guest of the Republic Day parade in New Delhi. France, was the first country, to sign a nuclear energy co-operation agreement, with India, during Prime Minister Singh's visit, following the waiver by the Nuclear Suppliers Group. During the Bastille Day celebrations on July 14, 2009, a detachment of 400 Indian troops marched along with the French troops as well as the Indian Prime Minister Dr. Manmohan Singh was the guest of honour.

Italy

Despite racial and religious disconnections, India and Italy have enjoyed overall pleasurable and strong relations throughout history. Italy and India are also close economic partners and is home to a large population of Indian immigrants. The chief of India's leading political party, The Indian National Congress, Sonia Gandhi, arguably the most powerful Indian woman, is of Italian descent. Unfortunately at diplomatic level the relations seem not to be always good, an example is the terrible visa situation between the two countries for the past few years, visas of any kind (tourist, business, employment and others) are issued for very short term and after a lot of hurdles for both Indian and Italian nationals.

This situation has reduced noticeably the possibility of tourism and business development between the two countries. It is not officially known the reason for the current diplomatic situation. India has an embassy in Rome, a general consulate in Milan. Italy has an embassy in New Delhi, 2 general consulates (in Mumbai and Calcutta). There are around 100,000 people of Indian Origin living in Italy, meanwhile there are only around 300 Italian citizens residing in India mostly working on behalf of Italian industrial groups.

Germany

During the Cold War India maintained diplomatic relations with West Germany and East Germany. Since the Fall of the Berlin wall, and the reunification of Germany, relations have further improved. The German ambassador to India, Bernd Mutzelburg, once said that India and Germany, are not just 'natural partners', but important countries in a globalised world. Germany is India's largest trade partner in Europe. German Chancellor, Angela Merkel visited India recently, as did the Indian Prime Minister Manmohan Singh visit Germany. Both countries have been working towards gaining permanent seats in the United Nations Security Council.

As both countries are strong liberal democracies, they have similar objectives. UN reforms, fighting terrorism and climate change, and promotion of science, education, technology, and human rights, are some areas of shared interests, and collaboration between these two countries. Culturally too, Indian and German writers and philosophers, have influenced each other. Recently, Germany has invested in developing education and skills amongst rural Indians.

Turkey

Due to controversial issues such as Turkey's close relationship with Pakistan and India's strong relations with Greece and Armenia, relations between the two countries have often been blistered at certain times, but better at others. India and Turkey's relationship alters from unsureness to collaboration when the two nations work together to combat terrorism in Central and South Asia, and the Middle East. India and Turkey are also connected by history, seeing as they've known each other since the days of the Ottoman Empire, and seeing as India was one of the countries to send aid to Turkey following its war of independence.

Estonia

Estonia–India relations India's first recognition of Estonia came on 22 September 1921 when the former had just acquired membership in the League of Nations. India re-recognised Estonia on September 9, 1991 and diplomatic relations were established on December 2 of the same year in Helsinki. Neither country has a resident ambassador. Estonia is represented in India by 2 honorary consulates (in Mumbai and New Delhi). India is represented in Estonia through its embassy in Helsinki (Finland) and through an honorary consulate in Tallinn.

Iceland

Iceland and India established diplomatic relations in 1972. The Embassy of Iceland in London was accredited to India and the Embassy of India in Oslo, Norway, was accredited to Iceland. However, it was only after 2003 that the two countries have began close diplomatic and economic relationships. In 2003, President of Iceland Ólafur Ragnar Grímsson visited India on diplomatic mission. This was the first visit by an Icelandic President to India. During the visit, Iceland pledged support to New Delhi's candidature for a permanent seat in the United Nation Security Council thus becoming the first Nordic country to do so. This was followed by an official visit of President of India A. P. J. Abdul Kalam to Iceland in May 2005. Following this a new embassy of Iceland was opened in New Delhi on 26 February 2006. Soon, a Indian Navy team visited Iceland on friendly mission. Gunnar Pálsson is the ambassador of Iceland to India. The Embassy's area of accreditation, apart from India includes Bangladesh, Indonesia, the Seychelles, Singapore, Sri Lanka, Malaysia, Maldives, Mauritius and Nepal. India appointed S. Swaminathan as the first resident ambassador to Iceland in March 2008.

Ireland

Indo-Irish relations picked up steam during the freedom struggles of the respective countries against a common imperial empire in the United Kingdom. Political relations between the two states have largely been based on socio-cultural ties, although political and economic ties have also helped build relations. Indo-Irish relations were greatly strengthened by the such luminaries as the likes of Pandit Nehru, Éamon de Valera, Rabindranath Tagore, W. B. Yeats, James Joyce, and, above all, Annie Besant. Politically relations have not been cold nor warm. Mutual benefit has led to economic ties that are fruitful for both states. Visits by government leaders have kept relations cordial at regular intervals.

Malta

Malta opened a High Commission in New Delhi in 2007. Malta also has an honourary consulate in Bombay. India is represented in Malta through its embassy in Tripoli, Libya and an honorary consulate in Valletta.

Ukraine

Diplomatic relations between India and Ukraine were established in January 1992. Indian Embassy in Kiev was opened in May 1992 and Ukraine opened its Mission in New Delhi in February 1993. The Consulate General of

India in Odessa functioned from 1962 till its closure in March 1999.

Poland

India–Poland relations Historically, relations have generally been close and friendly, characterized by understanding and cooperation on international front.

Arab States of the Persian Gulf

India and the Arab states of the Persian Gulf enjoy strong cultural and economic ties. This is reflected in the fact that more than 50% of the oil consumed by India comes from the Persian Gulf countries and Indian nationals form the largest expatriate community in the Arabian peninsula. The annual remittance by Indian expatriates in the region amounted to US$20 billion in 2007. India is one of the largest trading partners of the CCASG with non-oil trade between India and Dubai alone amounting to US$19 billion in 2007. The Persian Gulf countries have also played an important role in addressing India's energy security concerns, with Saudi Arabia and Kuwait regularly increasing their oil supply to India to meet the country's rising energy demand. In 2005, Kuwait increased its oil exports to India by 10% increasing the net oil trade between the two to US$4.5 billion. In 2008, Qatar decided to invest US$5 billion in India's energy sector. India has maritime security arrangement in place with Oman and Qatar, In 2008, a landmark defense pact was signed, under which India committed its military assets to protect "Qatar from external threats".

Bahrain

India is a close ally of Bahrain, the Kingdom along with its GCC partners are (according to Indian officials) among the most prominent backers of India's bid for a permanent seat on the UN Security Council, and Bahraini officials have urged India to play a greater role in international affairs. For instance, over concerns about Iran's nuclear programme Bahrain's Crown Prince appealed to India to play an active role in resolving the crisis.

Ties between India and Bahrain go back generations, with many of Bahrain's most prominent figures having close connections: poet and constitutionalist Ebrahim Al-Arrayedh grew up in Bombay, while 17th century Bahraini theologians Sheikh Salih Al-Karzakani and Sheikh Ja'far bin Kamal al-Din were influential figures in the Kingdom of Golkonda and the development of Shia thought in the sub-continent.

Bahraini politicians have sought to enhance these long standing ties, with Parliamentary Speaker Khalifa Al Dhahrani in 2007 leading a delegation of parliamentarians and business leaders to meet Indian President Pratibha Patil, opposition leader L K Advani, and take part in training and media interviews. Politically, it is easier for Bahrain's politicians to seek training and advice from India than it is from the United States or other western alternative.

In December 2007, the Bahrain India Society was launched in Manama to promote ties between the two countries. Headed by the former Minister of Labour Abdulnabi Al Shoala, the Society seeks to take advantage of the development in civil society to actively work to strengthen ties between the two countries, not only business links, but according to the body's opening statement in politics, social affairs, science and culture. India's Minister of State for Foreign Affairs E Ahmed and his Bahraini counterpart Dr Nazar Al Baharna attended the launch.

Egypt

In historical perspective, modern Egypt-India relations go back to the contacts between Saad Zaghloul and Mohandas Gandhi on the common goals of their respective movements of independence. In 1955, Egypt under Gamal Abdul Nasser and India under Jawaharlal Nehru became the founders of the Non-Aligned Movement. During the 1956 War, Nehru stood supporting Egypt to the point of threatening to withdraw his country from the British Commonwealth. In 1967, following the Arab-Israeli war, India supported Egypt and the Arabs. In 1977, New Delhi described the visit of President Anwar al-Sadat to Jerusalem as a "brave" move and considered the peace treaty between Egypt and Israel a primary step on the path of a just settlement of the Middle East problem. Major Egyptian exports to India include raw cotton, raw and manufactured fertilizers, oil and oil products, organic and non-organic chemicals, leather and iron products. Major imports into Egypt from India are cotton yarn, sesame, coffee, herbs, tobacco, lentils, pharmaceutical products and transport equipment. The Egyptian Ministry of Petroleum is also currently negotiating the establishment of a natural gas-operated fertilizer plant with another Indian company. In 2004 the Gas Authority of India Limited, bought 15% of Egypt Nat Gas distribution and marketing company. In 2008 Egyptian investment in India was worth some 750 million dollars, according to the Egyptian ambassador.

Iran

After the Iranian Revolution of 1979, Iran withdrew from CENTO and dissociated itself from US-friendly countries, including Pakistan, which automatically entailed improved relationship with the Republic of India.

Currently, the two countries have friendly relations in

many areas. There are significant trade ties, particularly in crude oil imports into India and diesel exports to Iran. Iran frequently objected to Pakistan's attempts to draft anti-India resolutions at international organizations such as the OIC. India welcomed Iran's inclusion as an observer state in the SAARC regional organization. Lucknow continues to be a major centre of Shiite culture and Persian study in the subcontinent.

In the 1990s, India and Iran both supported the Northern Alliance in Afghanistan against the Taliban regime. They continue to collaborate in supporting the broad-based anti-Taliban government led by Hamid Karzai and backed by the United States.

Iraq

Iraq was one of the few countries in the Middle East with which India established diplomatic relations at the embassy level immediately after its independence in 1947. Both nations signed the "Treaty of Perpetual Peace and Friendship" in 1952 and an agreement of cooperation on cultural affairs in 1954. India was amongst the first to recognize the Baath Party-led government, and Iraq remained neutral during the Indo-Pakistani War of 1965. However, Iraq sided alongside other Persian Gulf states in supporting Pakistan against India during the Indo-Pakistani War of 1971, which saw the creation of Bangladesh. The eight-year long Iran–Iraq War caused a steep decline in trade and commerce between the two nations. During the 1991 Persian Gulf War, India remained neutral but permitted refueling for U.S. airplanes. It opposed U.N. sanctions on Iraq, but the period of war and Iraq's isolation further diminished India's commercial and diplomatic ties. From 1999 onwards, Iraq and India began to work towards a stronger relationship. Iraq had supported India's right to conduct nuclear tests following its tests of five nuclear weapons on May 11 and May 13, 1998. In 2000, the then-Vice President of Iraq Taha Yassin Ramadan visited India, and on August 6, 2002 President Saddam Hussein conveyed Iraq's "unwavering support" to India over the Kashmir dispute with Pakistan.

India and Iraq established joint ministerial committees and trade delegations to promote extensive bilateral cooperation. Although initially disrupted during the 2003 invasion of Iraq, diplomatic and commercial ties between India and the new democratic government of Iraq have since been normalized.

Israel

Notably, the creation of Israel at the end of World War II was a complex issue. India, along with Iran and Yugoslavia had recommended a single state with Arab and Jewish majority provinces with an aim to prevent partition of historic Palestine and prevent any conflict that might follow based on its own experience during partition. However, the final UN resolution decided to partition historic Palestine into Arab and Jewish states based on religious and ethnic majority which India opposed in the final vote as it did not agree with concept of partition on the basis of religion. However, due to the security threat from a US aided Pakistan and its nuclear program in the 80s, Israel and India started a clandestine relationship that involved cooperation between their respective intelligence agencies. Israel shared India's concerns about the growing danger posed by Pakistan and nuclear proliferation to Iran and other Arab states.

After the end of the Cold War, formal relations with Israel started improving significantly. Since the establishment of full diplomatic relations with Israel in 1992, India has improved its relation with the Jewish State. India is regarded as Israel's strongest ally in Asia, and Israel is India's second largest arms supplier. Both countries share common strategic interests to combat Pakistan based Terrorism and Nuclear proliferation concerns. India has entertained Israeli Prime Minister in a visit in 2003, and Israel has entertained Indian dignitaries such as Finance Minister Jaswant Singh in diplomatic visits. India and Israel collaborate extensively in scientific and technological endeavors. Israel's Minister for Science and Technology has expressed interest in collaborating with the Indian Space Research Organization (ISRO) towards utilizing satellites for better management of land and other resources. Israel has also expressed interest in participating in ISRO's Chandrayaan Mission involving an unmanned mission to the moon. On January 21, 2008 India successfully launched an Israeli spy satellite into orbit from Sriharikota space station in southern India.

Further, Israel and India share intelligence on terrorist groups. They have developed close defense and security ties since establishing diplomatic relations in 1992. Israel is India's second-biggest arms supplier, after Russia. India has bought more than $5 billion worth of Israeli equipment since 2002. In addition, Israel is training Indian military units and discussing an arrangement to give Indian commandos instruction in counter-terrorist tactics and urban warfare. In December 2008, Israel and India signed a memorandum to set up an Indo-Israel Legal Colloquium to facilitate discussions and exchange programs between judges and jurists of the two countries.

Lebanon

India has a peacekeeping force as part of the UN Interim Force in Lebanon (UNIFIL). One infantry battalion is deployed in Lebanon and about 900 personnel are stationed in the Eastern part of South Lebanon. The force also provided non-patrol aid to citizens.

Saudi Arabia

Bilateral relations between India and the Saudi Arabia have strengthened considerably owing to cooperation in regional affairs and trade. Saudi Arabia is the one of largest suppliers of oil to India, who is one of the top 7 trading partners and the 5th biggest investor in Saudi Arabia.

India and Saudi Arabia are actively cooperating in the field of science and technology. CSIR and the Saudi Arabian Standards Organisation (SASO) have an ongoing programme of technical cooperation (POC) since June 1993. Under this programme, Indian experts in different scientific areas, particularly in the field of measurement and calibration, are deputed to Saudi Arabia on regular basis. Similarly, several Saudi experts and have undergone advanced training in India. National Physical Laboratory has provided expertise and technology for two important SASO projects related to calibration and teleclock system. CSIR and the King Abdulaziz City for Science and Technology (KACST) signed a MoU for bilateral cooperation in 1997 and have an ongoing programme of cooperation, particularly in the field of space science, remote sensing and installation of Internet. Recently a three-member delegation from CSIR, NPL and CFTRI visited SASO during January 2004 and both sides agreed to renew the POC.

Russia and Central Asia

The collapse of the Soviet Union and the emergence of the Commonwealth of Independent States (CIS) had major repercussions for Indian foreign policy. Substantial trade with the former Soviet Union plummeted after the Soviet collapse and has yet to recover. Longstanding military supply relationships were similarly disrupted due to questions over financing, although Russia continues to be India's largest supplier of military systems and spare parts.

The relationship with USSR was tested (and proven) during the 1971 war with Pakistan, which led to the subsequent liberation of Bangladesh. Soon after the victory of the Indian Armed Forces, one of the foreign delegates to visit India was Admiral S.G. Gorshkov, Chief of the Soviet Navy. During his visit to Mumbai (Bombay) he came on board INS *Vikrant*. During a conversation with Vice Admiral Swaraj Prakash, Gorshkov asked the Vice Admiral, "Were you worried about a battle against the American carrier?" He answered himself: "Well, you had no reason to be worried, as I had a Soviet nuclear submarine trailing the American task force all the way into the Indian Ocean."

Russian Federation

India's ties with the Russian Federation are time-tested and based on continuity, trust and mutual understanding. There is national consensus in both the countries on the need to preserve and strengthen India-Russia relations and further consolidate the strategic partnership between the two countries. A Declaration on Strategic Partnership was signed between former Russian President and current Prime Minister Vladimir Putin and former Indian Prime Minister Atal Bihari Vajpayee in October 2000.

It is remarkable to note that Russia and India have decided not to renew the 1971 Indo-Soviet Peace and Friendship Treaty and have sought to follow what both describe as a more pragmatic, less ideological relationship.

Russian President Yeltsin's visit to India in January 1993 helped cement this new relationship. Ties have grown stronger with President Vladimir Putin's 2004 visit. The pace of high-level visits has since increased, as has discussion of major defence purchases. Russia, is working for the development of the Kudankulam nuclear plant, that will be capable of producing 1000 MW of electricity. Gazprom, is working for the development of oil and natural gas, in the Bay of Bengal. India and Russia, have collaborated extensively, on space technology. Other areas of collaboration include software, ayurveda, etc. India and Russia, have set a determination in increasing trade to $10 billion. Counter-terrorism techniques are also in place between Russia and India. In 2007 President Vladimir Putin was guest of honour at Republic Day celebration on 26 January 2007. The year 2008, has been declared by both countries as the Russia-India Friendship Year. Bollywood films are quite popular in Russia. The Indian public-sector oil company ONGC bought Imperial Energy in 2008. In December 2008, during President Medvedev's visit, to New Delhi, India and Russia, signed a nuclear energy co-operation agreement.

Armenia

The first contacts between both civilizations date back from 2,500 years ago, during the 5th century BC. In modern times, India recognized Armenia on December 26, 1991.

Kazakhstan

India, is working towards developing strong relations with this resource rich Central Asian country. The Indian oil company, Oil and Natural Gas Corporation, has got oil exploration and petroleum development grants in Kazakhstan. The two countries are collaborating in petrochemicals, information technology, and space technology. Kazakhstan has offered India five blocks for oil and gas exploration. India and Kazakhstan, are to set up joint projects in construction, minerals and metallurgy. India also signed four other pacts, including an extradition treaty, in the presence of President Prathibha Patil and her Kazakh counterpart Nursultan Nazarbayev. Kazakhastan will provide uranium and related products under the MoU between Nuclear Power Corp. of India and KazatomProm. These MoU also opens possibilities of joint exploration of uranium in Kazakhstan, which has the worlds' second largest reserves, and India building atomic power plants in the Central Asian country.

Mongolia

The relations between India and Mongolia are still at a nascent stage and Indo-Mongolian cooperation is limited to diplomatic visits, provision of soft loans and financial aid and the collaborations in the IT sector. India established diplomatic relations in December 1955. India was the first country outside the Soviet block to establish diplomatic relations with Mongolia. Since then, there have been treaties of mutual friendship and cooperation between the two countries in 1973, 1994, 2001 and 2004.

Tajikistan

Diplomatic relations were established India and Tajikistan following Tajikistan's independence from the 1991 dissolution of the Soviet Union, which had been friendly with India. Tajikistan occupies a strategically important position in Central Asia, bordering Afghanistan, the People's Republic of China and separated by a small strip of Afghan territory from Pakistan. India's role in fighting the Taliban and Al-Qaeda and its strategic rivalry with both China and Pakistan have made its ties with Tajikistan important to its strategic and security policies. Despite their common efforts, bilateral trade has been comparatively low, valued at USD 12.09 million in 2005; India's exports to Tajikistan were valued at USD 6.2 million and its imports at USD 5.89 million. India's military presence and activities have been significant, beginning with India's extensive support to the anti-Taliban Afghan Northern Alliance (ANA). India began renovating the Farkhor Air Base and stationed aircraft of the Indian Air Force there. The Farkhor Air Base became fully operational in 2006, and 12 MiG-29 bombers and trainer aircraft are planned to be stationed there. India is only the fourth nation after the U.S., Russia and Germany to have a military base in Central Asia.

Uzbekistan

The countries have some culture in common especially because of deep Turkic and Persian influences in the two countries. India has an embassy in Tashkent. Uzbekistan has an embassy in New Delhi.

Liberia

The bilateral relations between the Republic of India and the Republic of Liberia have expanded on growing bilateral trade and strategic cooperation. India is represented in Liberia through its embassy in Abidjan (Ivory Coast) and an active honorary consulate in Monrovia since 1984. Liberia was represented in India through its resident mission in New Delhi which subsequently closed due to budgetary constraints.

Côte d'Ivoire

The bilateral relations between the Republic of India and the Republic of Côte d'Ivoire have considerably expanded in recent years as India seeks to develop an extensive commercial and strategic partnership in the West African region . The Indian diplomatic mission in Abidjan was opened in 1979. Côte d'Ivoire opened its resident mission in New Delhi in September 2004. Both nations are currently fostering efforts to increase trade, investments and economic cooperation.

Nigeria

India has close relations with this oil rich West African country. Twenty percent of India's crude oil needs are met, by Nigeria. 40000 barrels per day of oil, is the amount of oil, that India receives from Nigeria. Trade, between these two countries stands at $875 million in 2005-2006. Indian companies have also invested in manufacturing, pharmaceuticals, iron ore, steel, information technology, and communications, amongst other things. Both India and Nigeria, are members of the Commonwealth of Nations, G-77, and the Non Aligned Movement. The Nigerian President, Olusegun Obasanjo was the guest of honour, at the Republic Day parade, in 1999, and the Indian Prime Minister Manmohan Singh, visited Nigeria in 2007, and addressed the Nigerian Parliament.

South Africa

India and South Africa, have always had strong relations. There is a large group of South Africans of Indian descent. Mahatma Gandhi, spent many years in South Africa, during which time, he fought for the rights of the ethnic Indians. Nelson Mandela was inspired by Gandhi. After India's independence, India was strongly against apartheid, and refused diplomatic relations while apartheid was conducted.

The two countries, now have close economic, political, and sports relations. Trade between the two countries grew from $3 million in 1992-1993 to $4 billion in 2005-2006, and aim to reach trade of $12 billion by 2010. One third of India's imports from South Africa is gold bullion. Diamonds, that are mined from South Africa, are polished in India. Nelson Mandela was awarded the Gandhi Peace Prize. The two countries are also members of the IBSA Dialogue Forum, with Brazil. India hopes to get large amounts of uranium, from resource rich South Africa, for India's growing civilian nuclear energy sector.

Sudan

Indo-Sudanese relations have always been characterized as longstanding, close, and friendly, even since the early development stages of their countries. The two nations established diplomatic relations shortly after India became known as one of the first Asian countries to recognize the newly independent African country. India and Sudan also share geographic and historical similarities, as well as economic interests. Both countries are former British colonies, and remotely border Saudi Arabia by means of a body of water. India and Sudan continue to have cordial relations, despite issues such as India's close relationship with Israel, India's solidarity with Egypt over border issues with Sudan, and Sudan's intimate bonds with Pakistan and Bangladesh. India is also a contributor of a hefty UN peacekeeping force in Darfur.

Non-Aligned Movement

Nonalignment had its origins in India's colonial experience and the nonviolent Indian independence struggle led by the Congress, which left India determined to be the master of its fate in an international system dominated politically by Cold War alliances and economically by Western capitalism. The principles of nonalignment, as articulated by Nehru and his successors, were preservation of India's freedom of action internationally through refusal to align India with any bloc or alliance, particularly those led by the United States or the Soviet Union; nonviolence and international cooperation as a means of settling international disputes. Nonalignment was a consistent feature of Indian foreign policy by the late 1940s and enjoyed strong, almost unquestioning support among the Indian elite.

The term "Non-Alignment" itself was coined by Indian Prime Minister Jawaharlal Nehru during his speech in 1954 in Colombo, Sri Lanka.

United Nations

As a founder member of the United Nations, India has been a firm supporter of the Purposes and Principles of the United Nations, and has made significant contributions to the furtherance and implementation of these noble aims, and to the evolution and functioning of its various specialized programmes. It stood at the forefront during the UN's tumultuous years of struggle against colonialism and apartheid, its struggle towards global disarmament and the ending of the arms race, and towards the creation of a more equitable international economic order.

At the very first session of the UN, India had raised its voice against colonialism and apartheid, two issues which have been among the most significant of the UN's successes in the last half century. India exulted in the UN's triumph, and saw in the UN's victory, a vindication of the policy relentlessly pursued by it from its initial days at the world forum. India has been a participant in all its peace-keeping operations including those in Korea, Egypt and Congo in earlier years and in Somalia, Angola and Rwanda in recent years. India has also played an active role in the deliberations of the United Nations on the creation of a more equitable international economic order. It has been an active member of the Group of 77, and later the core group of the G-15 nations. Other issues, such as environmentally sustainable development and the promotion and protection of human rights, have also been an important focus of India's foreign policy in international forums. See more

SAARC

Certain aspects of India's relations within the subcontinent are conducted through the South Asian Association for Regional Cooperation (SAARC). Its members are Afghanistan, Bangladesh, Bhutan, India, Maldives, Nepal, Pakistan, and Sri Lanka. Established in 1985, SAARC encourages cooperation in agriculture, rural development, science and technology, culture, health, population control, narcotics control and anti-terrorism.

SAARC has intentionally stressed these "core issues" and avoided more divisive political issues, although political dialogue is often conducted on the margins of SAARC meetings. In 1993, India and its SAARC partners signed an agreement to gradually lower tariffs within the region. Forward movement in SAARC has come to a standstill because of the tension between India and Pakistan, and the SAARC Summit originally scheduled for, but not held in, November 1999 has not been rescheduled. The Fourteenth SAARC Summit was held during 3 - 4 April 2007 in New Delhi.

World Trade Organization

Described by WTO chief Pascal Lamy as one of the organization's "big brothers", India was instrumental in bringing down the Doha round of talks in 2008. It has played an important role of representing as many as 100 developing nations during WTO summits.

International Disputes

It is pertinent to note that India's territorial disputes

with neighboring Pakistan and People's Republic of China have played a crucial role in its foreign policy. India is also involved in minor territorial disputes with neighboring Bangladesh, Nepal and Maldives. India currently maintains two manned stations in Antarctica but has made some unofficial territorial claims, this is yet to be clarified.

Currently, India is involved in the following international disputes:

Bangladesh

(a) 6.5 km of the border between India and Bangladesh remains to be demarcated.

(b) Dispute with Bangladesh over South Talpatti Island / New Moore in the Bay of Bengal.

(c) Ongoing discussions with Bangladesh to exchange 162 minuscule enclaves between the two.

Nepal

(a) Kalapani village of India is claimed by Nepal and Nawalparasi district of Nepal is claimed by India.

The dispute between India and Nepal involves about 75 km^2 of area in Kalapani, where China, India, and Nepal meet. Indian forces occupied the area in 1962 after China and India fought their border war. Three villages are located in the disputed zone: Kuti Gunji, and Knabe. India and Nepal disagree about how to interpret the 1816 Sugauli Treaty between the British East India Company and Nepal, which delimited the boundary along the Maha Kali River (Sarda River in India). The dispute intensified in 1997 as the Nepali parliament considered a treaty on hydro-electric development of the river. India and Nepal differ as to which stream constitutes the source of the river. Nepal regards the Limpiyadhura as the source; India claims the

Lipu Lekh. Nepal has reportedly tabled an 1856 map from the British India Office to support its position. The countries have held several meetings about the dispute and discussed jointly surveying to resolve the issue. Although the Indo-Nepali dispute appears to be minor, it was aggravated in 1962 by tensions between China and India. Because the disputed area lies near the Sino-Indian frontier, it gains strategic value.

Maldives

(a) Dispute over Minicoy Island with Maldives.

(b) India prevented Maldives destabilization by armed rebels by executing Operation Cactus and restored law and order in Maldives.

Anglo Indian Ocean Territories

(1) Dispute over the British Indian Ocean Territories and the Cocos (Keeling) Islands with the former colonial powers. India regards these islands as part of its Lakshadweep Indosphere strategy as part of its oceanic vicinity of its sovereignty and a threat to its integrity of its emerging geo-political might, and does not recognise the crown's rule over these "Indian" islands.

Pakistan

(a) The unresolved Kashmir dispute and the status of Kashmir with Pakistan, involving the Siachen Glacier, India claims the disputed territory from *Pakistan occupied Kashmir* (PoK).

(b) Boundary issues of the Ferozepur and Pathankot with the Government of Pakistan.

(c) Dispute over Kori Creek and the maritime boundary regarding the Rann of Kachchh area of India.

(d) Water-sharing problems with Pakistan over the Indus River (Wular Barrage). *(Indus Water Treaty)*

People's Republic of China

(a) India claims Aksai Chin and Trans-Karakoram Tract, as part of Jammu and Kashmir.

(b) China claims most of Arunachal Pradesh, a contested disputed territory of north-east India by not recognising the McMahon Line. The McMahon Line however, had originally stretched farther southward into Indian territory than India's current territorial claims north of the line. The boundary claim itself is therefore still in dispute as it could give more territorial advantage to either nation. In a sense, the line might not serve as an advantage to India's claim, as a more southward boundary could give China more territorial claim.

Two regions are claimed by both India and China. Aksai Chin is in the disputed territory of Kashmir, at the junction of India, Tibet and Pakistan-Occupied Kashmir. India claims the 38,000-square-kilometre territory, currently administered by China. Arunachal Pradesh is a state of India in the country's northeast, bordering on Bhutan, Myanmar and China. Though it is under Indian administration, China calls the 90,000-square-kilometre area as South Tibet. Also the boundary between the North Indian states of Himachal Pradesh and Uttarakhand with China's Tibet is not properly demarcated with some portions under de-facto administration of India.

Look East Policy

In the post cold war era, a significant aspect of India's foreign policy is the Look East Policy. During the cold war,

India's relations with its South East Asian neighbours was not very strong. After the end of the cold war, the government of India particularly realised the importance of redressing this imbalance in India's foreign policy. Consequently, the Narasimha Rao government in the early nineties of the last century unveiled the look east policy. Initially it focused on renewing political and economic contacts with the countries of East and South-East Asia.

At present, under the Look East Policy, the Government of India is giving special emphasis on the economic development of backward northeastern region of India taking advantage of huge market of ASEAN as well as of the energy resources available in some of the member countries of ASEAN like Myanmar. After the start of liberalization, it was a very strategic policy decision taken by the government in the foreign policy. To quote Prime Minister Manmohan Singh "it was also a strategic shift in India's vision of the world and India's place in the evolving global economy". The policy was given an initial thrust with the then Prime Minister Narasimha Rao visiting China, Japan, South Korea, Vietnam and Singapore and India becoming a important dialogue partner with ASEAN in 1992.

Since the beginning of this century, India has given a big push to this policy by becoming a summit level partner of ASEAN (2002) and getting involved in some regional initiatives such as the BIMSTEC and the Ganga Mekong Cooperation and now becoming a member of the East Asia Summit (EAS) in December, 2005.

India – ASEAN

India's interaction with ASEAN in the cold war era was very limited. India declined to get associated with

ASEAN in the 1960s when full membership was offered even before the grouping was formed. It is only with the formulation of the Look-East policy in the last decade (1992), India had started giving this region due importance in the foreign policy.

India became a sectoral dialogue partner with ASEAN in 1992, a full dialogue partner in 1995, a member of the ASEAN Regional Forum (ARF) in 1996, and a summit level partner (on par with China, Japan and Korea) in 2002.

It is pertinent to note that first India-ASEAN Business Summit was held at New Delhi in October 2002. The then Prime Minister A.B. Vajpayee addressed this meet and since then this business summit has become an annual feature before the India-ASEAN Summits, as a forum for networking and exchange of business experiences between policy makers and business leaders from ASEAN and India.

So far, four India-ASEAN Summits, first in 2002 at Phnom Penh (Cambodia), second in 2003 at Bali (Indonesia), third in 2004 at Vientiane (Laos) and the fourth in 2005 at Kuala Lumpur (Malaysia), have taken place.

The following agreements have been entered into with ASEAN:

(1) Framework Agreement on Comprehensive Economic Cooperation (for establishing a FTA in a time frame of 10 years) was concluded in Bali in 2003.

(2) An ASEAN-India Joint Declaration for Cooperation to Combat International Terrorism has been adopted.

(3) India has acceded to the Treaty of Amity and Cooperation (TAC) in 2003, on which ASEAN was formed initially (in 1967).

(4) Agreement on "India-ASEAN Partnership for Peace, Progress and Shared Prosperity" was signed at the 3rd ASEAN-India Summit in Nov 2004.

(5) Setting up of Entrepreneurship Development Centres in ASEAN member states – Cambodia, Myanmar, Laos and Vietnam.

The following proposals were announced by the Prime Minister at the 4th ASEAN-India Summit:

(1) Setting up centres for English Language Training (ELT) in Cambodia, Laos, Myanmar and Vietnam.

(2) Setting up a tele-medicine and tele-education network for Cambodia, Myanmar, Laos and Vietnam.

(3) Organising special training courses for diplomats from ASEAN countries.

(4) Organising an India-ASEAN Technology Summit in 2006.

(5) Organising education fairs and road shows in ASEAN countries.

(6) Conducting an India-ASEAN IT Ministerial and Industry Forum in 2006.

The ASEAN region has an abundance of natural resources and significant technological skills. These provide a natural base for the integration between ASEAN and India in both trade and investment. The present level of bilateral trade with ASEAN of nearly US $ 18 billion is reportedly increasing by about 25 % per year. It was reached the level of US $ 30 billion by 2007. India is also improving its relations with the help of other policy decisions like offers of lines of credit, better connectivity through air, rail and road links etc.

7

Foreign Relations of Bangladesh

Bangladesh is a country in South Asia. It is bordered by India on all sides except for a small border with Burma (Myanmar) to the far southeast and by the Bay of Bengal to the south. Together with the Indian state of West Bengal, it makes up the ethno-linguistic region of Bengal. The name *Bangladesh* means "Country of Bengal" in the official Bengali language.

The borders of present-day Bangladesh were established with the partition of Bengal and India in 1947, when the region became the eastern wing of the newly-formed Pakistan. However, it was separated from the western wing by 1,600 kilometres (1,000 mi) across India. Political and linguistic discrimination as well as economic neglect led to popular agitations against West Pakistan, which led to the war for independence in 1971 and the establishment of Bangladesh. After independence the new state endured famines, natural disasters and widespread poverty, as well as political turmoil and military coups. The restoration of democracy in 1991 has been followed by relative stability and economic progress.

In the context of international relatons Bangladesh pursues a moderate foreign policy that places heavy reliance on multinational diplomacy, especially at the United Nations.

BASIC FACTS	
Capital	Dhaka
Official languages	Bengali
Government	Parliamentary republic
– President	Zillur Rahman
– Prime Minister	Sheikh Hasina Wazed
Independence	from Pakistan
– Declared	March 26, 1971
– Victory Day	December 16, 1971
Area	
– Total	144,000 km2 (94th)55,599 sq mi
– Water (%)	7.0
Population	
– 2007 estimate	150,448,340 (7th)
– Density	1045/km2 (11th)2,706/sq mi
GDP (PPP)	2008 estimate
– Total	$224.889 billion (48th)
– Per capita	$1,389 (153rd)
GDP (nominal)	2008 estimate
– Total	$81.938 billion (58th)
– Per capita	$506 (157th)
Gini (2000)	31.8 (medium)
HDI (2008)	0.524 (medium) (147th)
Currency	Taka (BDT)
Time zone	BDT (UTC+6)
– Summer (DST)	not observed (UTC+6)
Drives on the	left
Internet TLD	.bd
Calling code	880

Commonwealth

Bangladesh joined the Commonwealth of Nations in

1972 and has actively participated in the Heads of Government conferences that occur bi-annually.

United Nations

Bangladesh was admitted to the United Nations in 1974 and was elected to a Security Council term in 1978-1980 and again for a 2000-2002 term. Foreign Minister Choudhury served as president of the 41st UN General Assembly in 1986. In recent years, Bangladesh has played a significant role in international peacekeeping activities. Several thousand Bangladeshi military personnel are deployed overseas on peacekeeping operations. Under UN auspices, Bangladeshi troops have served or are serving in Somalia, Rwanda, Mozambique, Kuwait, Bosnia, and Haiti, and units are currently serving in Kuwait and East Timor. Bangladesh responded quickly to President Clinton's 1994 request for troops and police for the multinational force for Haiti and provided the largest non-U.S. contingent. As of June 2008, Bangladesh is the second largest provider of UN peacekeepers.

Non Aligned Movement (NAM)

Bangladesh was slated to become the next chairman of NAM at the summit scheduled for Dhaka 2001, however it was later decided to host the summit at an alternative venue.

SAARC

The government also pursued the expansion of cooperation among the nations of South Asia, bringing the process—an initiative of former President Ziaur Rahman—through its earliest, most tentative stages to the formal inauguration of the South Asian Association for Regional Cooperation (SAARC) at a summit gathering of South Asian leaders in Dhaka in December 1985. Bangladesh has served in the chairmanship of SAARC and has participated in a wide range of ongoing SAARC regional activities.

Organization of the Islamic Conference

Following the recognition of Bangladesh by Pakistan in 1974, Sheikh Mujibur Rahman led a Bangladeshi delegation to the Organisation of the Islamic Conference (OIC) conference in Lahore upon which Bangladesh was admitted as a member. In 1977, the President Ziaur Rahman amended the Constitution of Bangladesh, including a clause stating that "the state shall endeavour to consolidate, preserve and strengthen fraternal relations among Muslim countries based on Islamic solidarity". Since then, an explicit goal of Bangladeshi foreign policy has been to seek close relations with other Islamic states. In 1983, Bangladesh hosted the foreign ministers meeting of the OIC.

Centre on Integrated Rural Development for Asia and the Pacific

An intergovernmental and autonomous organisation, the organisation consists of ten members:- Afghanistan, Bangladesh, India, Indonesia, Myanmar, Nepal, Pakistan, Philippines, Thailand and Vietnam. The area of cooperation is primarily focused on agriculture, regional relations and the development of the region.

Bay of Bengal Initiative for Multi-Sectoral Technical and Economic Cooperation

An international organisation which includes South Asian and Southeast Asian nations. The member nations of this group are: Bangladesh, India, Myanmar, Sri Lanka, Thailand, Bhutan and Nepal. The organisation focuses on regional economy, regional development and trade & investment.

Developing 8 Countries

Bangladesh along with the seven other nations are all original members and no plans for expansions have been made. The Developing 8 is an economic development alliance consisting of Muslim majority states which focuses in multiple areas which are rural development, science and technology, banking, agriculture, humanitarian development, energy, environment, health and finance. On May 14, 2006 in Bali, Indonesia Bangladesh was the only nation not to sign a preferential trade agreement.

Asia Pacific Trade Agreement (APTA)

In 2005, Bangladesh signed the APTA agreement which would enable it to reduce trade gaps between itself and other nations such as China, South Korea and its neighbour India. Another aspect of the agreement is to be given duty free access to its products.

Like Minded Group

Bangladesh have formed an alliance with nineteen other developing countries to vote as a block in organisations such as the WTO and the United Nations.

Other

Bangladesh is currently chairman of the Developing 8 Countries. The government has participated in numerous international conferences, especially those dealing with population, food, development, and women's issues. In 1982-83, Bangladesh played a constructive role as chairman of the "Group of 77," an informal association encompassing most of the world's developing nations. It has taken a leading role in the "Group of 48" developing countries. Bangladesh also participates in these international organizations: ARF, AsDB, BIMSTEC, CP, FAO, IAEA, IBRD, ICAO, ICC, ICCt (signatory), ICRM, IDA, IDB,

IFAD, IFC, IFRCS, IHO, ILO, IMF, IMO, Interpol, IOC, IOM, IPU, ISO, ITU, ITUC, MIGA, MINURSO, MONUC, SACEP, UNCTADUNESCO, UNHCR, UNIDO, UNMEE, UNMIL, UNMIS, UNOCI, UNOMIG, UNWTO, UPU, WCL, WCO, WFTU, WHO, WIPO, WMO, WTO, OPCW.

Bilateral Relations

Since Bangladesh is almost entirely encircled by India via a land border which stretches 2400 kilometers (1500 miles), its relations with India are vital. After the assassination of Sheikh Mujib Pakistan established full diplomatic relations with Bangladesh and announced an aid package while India's attitude cooled considerably. The relations are further complicated by the two main political parties supporting opposing sides: Secular Awami League has a relatively India-friendly platform while Islamist BNP has a pro-Pakistan platform (although BNP is primarily nationalist and more vocal about the 1971 Bangladesh atrocities).

With Kingdom of Bhutan

Along with India, Bangladesh is one of the only two nations to have a residential embassy in Bhutan. The relationship between Bhutan and Bangladesh have always been positive since 1971 when the former became the first country to recognise Bangladesh after gaining independence from Pakistan. Bhutan as well as Nepal see Bangladesh as another access to the sea and an opportunity to be less dependent on India and China. The business community in Bhutan are asking for more investment from Bangladesh after a meeting in the Federation of Chambers of Commerce and Industry (FBCCI) in Dhaka. Imports from Bhutan during the 07-08 fiscal year, Bhutan's imports were worth \$10.8 million whereas Bangladesh's exports to Bhutan was only worth \$0.78 million.

With Republic of India

At the outset India's relations with Bangladesh could not have been stronger because of India's unalloyed support for independence and opposition against Pakistan at the time. During the independence war, many refugees fled to India. India also intervened militarily and may have helped bring international attention to the issue through Indira Gandhi's visit to Washington, D.C. Afterwards India furnished relief and reconstruction aid. India extended recognition to Bangladesh prior to the end of the war in 1971 (the second country to do so after Bhutan) and subsequently lobbied others to follow suit. Indo-Bangladesh relations have been strained over the years over issues such as South Talpatti Island, the Tin Bigha corridor and access to Nepal, the Farakka Barrage and water sharing, border conflicts near Tripura and the construction of a fence along most of the border which India explains as security provision against migrants, insurgents and terrorists. Many Bangladeshis feel India likes to play "big brother" to smaller neighbors, including Bangladesh. Bilateral relations warmed in 1996, due to a softer Indian foreign policy and the new Awami League Government. A 30-year water-sharing agreement for the Ganges River was signed in December 1996, after an earlier bilateral water-sharing agreement for the Ganges River lapsed in 1988. Both nations also have cooperated on the issue of flood warning and preparedness.

The Bangladesh Government and tribal insurgents signed a peace accord in December 1997, which allowed for the return of tribal refugees who had fled into India, beginning in 1986, to escape violence caused by an insurgency in their homeland in the Chittagong Hill Tracts. The Bangladesh Army maintains a very strong presence in the area to this day. The army is increasingly concerned about a growing problem of cultivation of illegal drugs. There are also small pieces of land along the border region that Bangladesh is diplomatically trying to reclaim. Padua, part of Sylhet Division before 1971, has been under Indian control since the war in 1971. This small strip of land was re-occupied by the BDR in 2001, but later given back to India after Bangladesh government decided to solve the problem through diplomatic negotiations. South Talpatty island (called New Moor by India), administered under Satkhira district of Bangladesh, is still under Indian military occupation, though the Bangladesh government sent satellite images to the Indian government proving the island to be within Bangladeshi territory. In recent years India has increasingly complained that Bangladesh does not secure its border properly. It fears an increasing flow of economically depressed Bangladeshis and it accuses Bangladesh of harboring Indian separatist groups like ULFA and alleged terrorist groups. The Bangladesh government has consistently denied these accusations. India estimates that over 20 million Bangladeshis are living illegally in India. One Bangladeshi official responded that "there is not a single Bangladeshi migrant in India". Since 2002, India has been constructing an India - Bangladesh Fence along much of the 2500 mile border. But recent relations are not without bright spots. In May 2007 they announced that for the first time since the 1965 Indo-Pak War, rail service between Kolkata and Dhaka will be restored, a lapse of 42 years. Moreover in October 2007 some cooperation was announced on the border issues mentioned above.

These signs of cooperation coincide for the moment at least with a change in Bangladeshi leadership that is expected to last until the end of 2008.

With Maldives

As being two moderate Islamic states, both nations always considered their bilateral relations to be excellent. Maldives as a nation dependent on its tourism sector, they have asked Bangladesh to export manpower to the island state. At the 15th SAARC Summit, Maldives and Bangladesh met at the sidelines to discuss the possibility of sending more semi-skilled and skilled workers. There are already 40,000 workers in Maldives mostly in unskilled and semi-skilled jobs.

With Federal Democratic Republic of Nepal

Nepal has good bilateral relations with Bangladesh as they view the latter nation as a great access to the sea giving them the opportunity to develop potential transit and trade facilities and be less dependent on India and China. Nepal recognised Bangladesh on 16 January, 1972 and relations further improved after the military coup on August 1975. The turning point for the two nations occurred in April 1976, signing a four-point agreement on technical cooperation, trade, transit and civil aviation. They both seek cooperation in the fields of power generation and development of water resources. In 1986, relations further improved when Bangladesh insisted Nepal should be included on a deal regarding the distribution of water from the Ganges River.

With Pakistan

The Bangladesh-Pakistan relationship is yet to be at a level that may be called warm. However since full diplomatic relations were implemented in January 1976, it has shown improvement in bilateral relations concerning commerce, culture and trade and making reconciliatory agreements.

Landmarks in their reconciliation are:

(a) An August 1973 agreement between Bangladesh and Pakistan on the repatriation of numerous individuals, including 90,000 Pakistani prisoners of war stranded in Bangladesh as a result of the 1971 conflict;

(b) A February 1974 accord by Bangladesh and Pakistan on mutual diplomatic recognition, followed more than 2 years later by establishment of formal diplomatic relations on January 18th 1976

(c) The organization by the UN High Commissioner for Refugees (UNHCR) of an airlift that moved almost 250,000 Bengalis from Pakistan to Bangladesh, and non-Bengalis from Bangladesh to Pakistan; and

(d) Exchanges of high-level visits, including a visit by Prime Minister Benazir Bhutto to Bangladesh in 1989 and visits by Prime Minister Khaleda Zia to Pakistan in 1992 and in 1995.

The following issues need resolving:

(1) Division of assets from the pre-1971 period

(2) Repatriation of 250,000 ethnic Biharis known as "Stranded Pakistanis"

(3) Possibly the most important and most sensitive issue is the Question of Pakistan's apology for the genocide in 1971 which has lead to the break down of numerous talks between the two.

With Sri Lanka

Relations are historically tied together even beyond the sub-continent's colonisation by the British. Sri Lanka's first King (to be mentioned in the ancient Pali chronicles) was alleged to have ancestors from the Vanga Kingdom which occupied an area now known as Bangladesh. Bangladesh's Buddhist minority gifted Sri Lanka with a few strands of hair said to have belonged to Buddha as a sign of goodwill. It is a worshipped object on Poya Day, a Buddhist public holiday in Sri Lanka.

Notably, in August 2008, both Heads of States discussed the implementation of new air links in hope of increasing trade, investment and stronger cultural links. Sri Lanka's current investments have been in Bangladesh's garment and banking sector and expect to diversify into different areas. Bangladesh also hosts a number of Sri Lankan medical students and cricket as a form of friendly communications between their people. There has been discussion to increase bilateral relations, cooperation between the two navies and sending Sri Lankan Naval personal to study in Bangladesh.

With State of Brunei

Bilateral relations are excellent between the two predominantly moderate Muslim nations. They are both members of OIC, Commonwealth and NAM and share common views on regional and international issues. Brunei recognised Bangladesh quickly with other Southeast Asian countries (Muslim majority nations like Indonesia and Malaysia in particular) and Bangladesh established residential Diplomatic mission in 1985, although they closed it down in 1988 due to financial constraints. In 1997, Bangladesh reopened its embassy, Brunei has a residential embassy located in Dhaka. Brunei actively supports Bangladesh's candidacy for different regional and international organisations. They supported Bangladesh's United Nation Economic and Social Council 2004-06 tenure, UNESCO Executive Board from 2003-07, Governing Board of the ASEAN Organization of the Supreme Audit Institution

(ASOSAI) for the 2004-06 term and membership into the ASEAN Regional Forum (ARF).

Both countries are looking to increase trade & investment such as Bangladesh's pharmaceutical products and Brunei's oil in particular. Brunei also imports manpower from Bangladesh although recently Bangladesh have been asking to take in more manpower especially professionals and to reduce the price of applying to work in Brunei by half (currently it is $1800 per worker from South Asian countries). Education is another part of their relations such as the Brunei Darussalam Government Scholarship for Commonwealth Countries. One Bangladeshi student who wins this scholarship has the opportunity to study at University of Brunei Darussalam (UBD) and Institute Technology Brunei (ITB) to stuay science based subjects. Students in Brunei have also been able to go to Bangladesh to study at their Medical Colleges and other higher education institutions offering quality education in Asia at a lower cost compared to western nations.

Defence relations is improving although Bangladesh are expecting more trainee officers in the future. Every year Brunei sends its personal for training in Defence Services Command and Staff College and other Military institutions. Defence officers from Bangladesh can also visit Military institutions in Brunei although it is only optional. Both countries have agreed to increase air links between the two countries which have already signed two agreements in 2004 and 2006 resulting in Bangladesh granting 5th freedom traffic rights with "intermediate" and "beyond" like Singapore and Dubai. With such proposed links it could be possible to not only connect Bangladeshis abroad to travel back home more easily, it can also help attract investors from Brunei for the tourism sector.

Both countries have setup a joint committee primarily to discuss the current bilateral relations and how it can improve although they can discuss international issues with mostly similar views on.

With Cambodia

Bangladesh signed trade agreement on August 4, 2006 with Cambodia in Phnom Penh. The trade agreement will help in further expanding and strengthening trade relations between the two countries. Bangladesh's major export items to Cambodia are readymade garment, footwear and leather goods, knitwear, pharmaceuticals, table wear, home linen, textile, seafood and marine products, tea, potato, jute and jute goods, light engineering products, spices, cosmetics, ceramic, melamine products and toiletries. Major import items from Cambodia are—cotton, edible oil, fertilizer, clinker, staple fiber, yarn and capital machinery.

With Indonesia

Both being moderate Muslim majority states, relations are considered excellent. Indonesia along with other non-Arab Muslim countries such as Malaysia, Turkey and Afghanistan immediately recognised Bangladesh. Relations have gone into different areas such as trade & investment, cultural exchange and peacekeeping. Both have similar views on international issues as being members of both Developing 8 and OIC. Indonesia have recently signed a deal with a pharmaceutical company called Eskayef Bangladesh Ltd. to export its goods to their country where Bangladesh sees another potential market for its pharmaceutical products.

With Malaysia

As two predominantly Muslim nations known for their tolerance and religious moderation, the two nations share an excellent relationship. Malaysia was one of the first Muslim states along with Indonesia to recognise Bangladesh and since then the two have seen a rapid growth of cooperation between them. Malaysia offers economic and technical assistance, trade and investment while Bangladesh offers a cheap labour workforce for areas such as construction.

In fact, Malaysia is the largest ASEAN investor in Bangladesh and Malaysian companies have invested $1.3 billion in 59 projects in 2007 in areas such as telecommunications, textiles and financial sector. However the trade balance is overwhelmingly in Malaysia's favour, during the 2006-07 fiscal year, exports were a mere $16.9 million compared to $384.16 million in imports. Trading between the two nations are increasing especially in pharmaceutical exports with a number businesses are calling for a Free Trade Agreement to balance out the trade deficit. Many Malaysian companies have shown keen interest to participate in infrastructure projects here such as power generation, sea port development, waste disposal system, construction of roads and highways as well as in the service sector such as education and healthcare.

Malaysia said will continue to contribute positive efforts to promote and expand bilateral relations with Bangladesh, particularly in trade and investment. Pending projects like the Dhaka-Chittagong highway, worth $1.2 billion, power generation, port development etc. would be completed. Malaysia and Bangladesh recently agreed to signing a Memorandum of Understanding in a tackle against money laundering from Bangladesh to Malaysia. The signatories are the financial intelligence units of the central banks from both nations with one aspect of the deal being that any Bangladeshi comes under suspicion they will gain information from Malaysia freely. Bangladesh and Malaysia are also members of Developing 8, OIC, Commonwealth, Like Minded Group and Non-Aligned Movement show that the two have similar views on regional and international issues. Issue of labor force administration in Malaysia has somewhat strained the bilateral ties temporarily. In 2007 Malaysia banned imports of Bangladeshi workers into the country after hundreds of them were stranded at an airport because their employers failed to collect them.

There were demonstrations in Kuala Lumpur by Bangladeshi workers demanding payments and better conditions. This created a crisis in the bilateral ties but issue has been resolved with the interference of the governments.

With Myanmar

Bilateral ties with Myanmar are good, despite occasional border strains and an influx of more than 270,000 Muslim refugees (known as "Rohingya") from predominantly Buddhist Burma. As a result of bilateral discussions, and with the cooperation and assistance of the UNHCR, most of the Rohingya refugees have now returned to Burma. As of 2000, about 22,000 refugees remain in camps in southern Bangladesh.

At the 2008 ASEAN Regional forum summit in Singapore, Bangladesh and Myanmar have pledged to solve their maritime border disputes as quickly as possible especially that a UN deadline in claiming maritime territories will expire in three years time. Both countries discussed the possibility of linking the two countries together in an attempt to boost their trade and commerce relations. The estimate to complete the 25km highway is three years and at the cost of $20 million. Another aspect of this plan is to connect the highway to the Asian Superhighway which would connect the two countries to China.

With Thailand

Relations are considered close and cordial and have made strides to improve trade and investment between the two countries. Diplomatic relations were established on October 5, 1972 and Thailand opened its embassy in 1974 followed by Bangladesh setting up their own in Bangkok in the following year. The first visit between the two countries was President Ziaur Rahman's visit to Thailand in 1979 followed by Prime Minister Prem Tinsulanond in 1983. Other Heads of States like Ershad visited in 1985, 1988 and 1990 and Thaksin Shinawatra in July and December 2002 and January 2004. Thailand is a key country in Bangladesh's "Look East" policy and relations have begun to increase and diversify into different areas. They seek not to intervene in each others internal matters as shown by their response to the events occurring in their own respective countries in 2006 such as the 2006 Thai coup d'état and 2006–2008 Bangladeshi political crisis. Both have considerable cooperation in summits organised by BIMSTEC and the ASEAN regional forum. Upper class and upper middle class Bangladeshis often go to Thailand for medical treatment and operations that the country's medical infrastructure cannot provide.

With Vietnam

After Bangladesh gained independence in 1971, it had strongly supported North Vietnam's struggle with the US and strongly opposed the bombing of North Vietnam which was demonstrated by nation-wide movements. Bangladesh was the first South Asian and second Asian nation to establish relations with South Vietnam at an ambassadorial level. On 11 February 1973, both nations officially established diplomatic relations. In 1982, Vietnam closed its embassy in Dhaka for financial reasons and reopened it in January 2003. Bangladesh opened its embassy in Ha Noi in November 1993. Relations between the nations are good and had been marked with several high level visits such as Khaleda Zia's visit in 2005 and President Tran Duc Luong in 2004. They maintain good cooperation on an international level in organisations such as the United Nations, Non-Aligned Movement and ASEAN regional forum. Bangladesh has supported Vietnam as a candidate for a non-permanent seat in the UN Security Council.

With North Korea

Due to their pro-China administration, North Korea did not establish ties until China recognised and established relations with Bangladesh in 1974. There is a North Korean embassy located in Dhaka although Bangladesh maintains a non-residential status. Instead communication between the Juche state and Bangladesh is with the latter's embassy in Beijing. Relations have only gone as far as recognition and neither nation has ever desired to progress this even further, especially due to the increase in military cooperation between Bangladesh and South Korea and North Korea's isolationist policies. In 2006, Bangladesh have used its ties with North Korea, urging them to comply with a UN resolution after North Korea's missile launch during a meeting with then Japanese Foreign Minister, Taro Aso.

With South Korea

Relations are considered to be productive and progressive. Their relations have gone on to expand in several areas such as defence and trade & investment. Bangladesh also sends a large number of skilled migrant workers to South

Korea to work in the following sectors:- construction, manufacture, services, and agriculture, fisheries and livestock. Bangladesh and South Korea's Olympic organisations signed an agreement which would benefit Bangladesh's sports development. One aspect is to bring in highly skilled Korean coaches to train Bangladeshi athletes and exchange of sport teams. South Korea and Bangladesh are also increasing military ties, such as joint military exercises, training of units such as special forces and building a submarine. Bangladesh has already procured a ULSAN class frigate from South Korea.

With People's Republic of China

Early relations with the People's Republic of China were cold due to the rare use of China's veto at the United Nations Security Council to block Bangladesh's accession to the United Nations. Lately however China has made efforts to improve relations with many of its neighbors. Trade with China reached a record level in 2006 of $3.2 billion under the auspices of the Asia-Pacific Trade Agreement (AFTA). The trade balance between the two countries are in China's favour. China has also officially agreed to helping Bangladesh on developing their nuclear power plant. Bangladesh has also signed the Apsco convention with six other nations to form a pact with China on space exploration.

With Republic of China

There is no choice available recognising both the PRC and ROC as legitimate nations, so Bangladesh opted to recognise the PRC. However, there is unofficial diplomatic relations with a ROC representative office in Dhaka. Although Bangladesh does not recognise the ROC (therefore illegal to travel there with a Bangladeshi passport), it quietly lifted a ban on flights between Dhaka and Taiwan.

With Kyrgyz Republic

Bangladesh established diplomatic relations with Kyrgyzstan immediately after the Collapse of the Soviet Union in 1992. As Bangladesh had mutual relations with the Soviet Union, the former intended to increase cooperation after the collapse, especially amongst the new Muslim majority nations. As Bangladesh have begun increasing production of pharmaceutical goods, melamine, garments and jute products other nations have become increasingly interested such as Kyrgyzstan who's Ambassodor Orolbaeva Irina Abdyevna have said this could help strengthen bilateral ties. Other areas including education have been mentioned, with a demand of increasing educational exchange. President Iajuddin Ahmed had said with the increasing standards of higher education especially in engineering, medical, science and technology, he stated Kyrgyz students can benefit studying in Bangladesh's educational facilities. Kyrgyzstan's expertise in hydoelectricity can also help with Bangladesh's growing energy problem.

Bangladesh's presence in Africa is mostly due to their large contribution to the peacekeeping forces present around the continent such as Liberia, Sierra Leone, Ivory Coast, Sudan (Darfur) and Somalia. Bangladesh can foster ties based on its history such as nations in East Africa where there is a South Asian population (whose ancestors immigrated there during the British Empire) and as a Muslim majority country it can develop ties easily with nations in North Africa, Sudan and Nigeria. In countries such as Ivory Coast and Sierra Leone, Bangladeshi peacekeepers have been honoured. In Sierra Leone, Bengali have been declared a state language. It is currently trying to increase ties with the southern economic bloc in Southern Africa with nations such as Zimbabwe.

With Arab Republic of Egypt

Bangladesh and Egypt being Islamic states and sharing same views on international policies such as the occupation of Palestine and being members of D-8, OIC and the Like Minded Group have helped to strengthen relations. Areas which the two countries are involved in are primarily trade, agro-processing, pharmaceuticals, science, technology and tourism. There is also a number of Bangladeshi students studying in Egypt and Bangladesh have asked to accept more through its scholarship programme. Egypt also imports semi-skilled and skilled manpower from the South Asian country. However, along with increasing cooperation in education, they also want Egypt to accept more workers.

With Great Socialist People's Libyan Arab Jamahiriya

Relations between the two were non-existent due to the refusal to recognise Bangladesh and granting asylum to some of those who assassinated Sheikh Mujib. After Bangladesh began sending its diplomats to the Arab world such as Libya to explain their view of the war, they immediately recognised and established diplomatic relations with Bangladesh. Bangladesh opened its embassy in Tripoli on January 8th, 1975. Cooperation between the two countries are primarily in international foras such as the UN and the OIC. Both nations have a low-key relations but are generally good due to common grounds of social values and religion.

They are now considering to increase trade ties such as importing Bangladesh's pharmaceutical products and Libyan oil. Bangladesh have asked Libya to ease visa restrictions for Bangladesh nationals and to take in more manpower. Apart from labourers there are also Bangladeshis working in professional occupations increasing people to people links.

Bangladesh have also welcomed Libyan students to study engineering and medical degrees at their universities. There has also been discussion to set up a joint committee to increase bilteral trade. Bangladesh is an accredited mission to Tunisia and Malta and uses its embassy in Libya to communicate with those countries.

With Republic of South Africa

Relations began during the inauguration of Nelson Mandela in 1994, and full diplomatic relations were implemented on 10 September, 1994.

Notably, due to the brutality and the White Supremacist ideology of the Apartheid regime, relations between South Africa and Bangladesh were non-existent until the collapse of white minority rule and Nelson Mandela's rise to power. There is a number of Bangladeshis which make up the South Asian community in South Africa and immigration still continues, although it has temporarily halted due to attacks against foreign workers. Bangladesh exports its raw materials such as leather, finished jute and also garments and textiles. South Africa exports to Bangladesh are iron ore, steel, aluminium, infrastructure projects and machinery and equipment for railways.

With Sudan

Throughout the course of history, relations between Bangladesh and Africa's largest country by size have been generally warm and strong. Seeing as both nations share a common religion, relations are generally good, but only recently has cooperation began to increase between the two countries. In March 2008, both governments came to an agreement which would primarily allow Bangladesh to export semi-skilled and skilled workers and also the opportunity to allow Bangladeshi firms and companies to expand their operations to Sudan which is now enjoying an oil boom regardless of the events occurring in Darfur.

As part of their growing relation, it is reported there would be an inauguration ceremony for Bangladesh's Diplomatic mission in Khartoum. Relations have diverged into different areas such as education where Sudan has offered more scholarships to Bangladeshi students and recently Sudan has shown interest in importing pharmaceuticals from Bangladesh. Bangladesh agreed to sending 1,600 of its personal and urgently needed helicopters to join the UN peacekeeping force in Darfur.

With Tanzania

Like other countries in East Africa, they share historical and religious ties to the former British Indian nations such as Pakistan, India and Bangladesh. Tanzania has a South Asian community due to the immigration of Indian clerical workers to Africa during the time of the British Empire. Tanzania has recently decided to import pharmaceutical goods from a Bangladeshi company known as Square Pharma. Tanzania was originally heavily dependent on India and other MNCs for medicines.

Middle East

It is remarkable that during the Bangladesh Liberation War, West Pakistan began a domestic and international propaganda campaign about the situation whereas India began its own media campaign in defense of the pro-independence faction. Because India was considered a non-Muslim nation, the majority of conservative Arab nations were in support of Pakistan, although interestingly enough non-Arab Muslim nations such as Indonesia and Turkey sympathised and established relations quickly. In the present, Bangladesh maintains relations to the Middle East through many areas such as commerce, history, military and most importantly religious ties which enabled the two to cooperate more easily then compared to their Western or Far Eastern partners. Bangladesh supplies over 1 million guest workers to Saudi Arabia, United Arab Emirates, Kuwait and other Gulf countries. In turn most of Bangladesh's oil is imported from this region. Islamic countries and charities provide economic aid usually to advance the Islamic agenda, including funding mosques and madrassas. During the Yom Kippur War, Bangladesh supported the Arabs and Palestinians and sent a medical team and relief supply which was appreciated. In return they enabled Bangladesh to become a member of NAM at the Algiers Summit in 1973 and pressured Pakistan into recognising Bangladesh in order to get Mujib to go to the 1974 OIC Summit in Lahore, as he stated that was his only condition.

Bangladesh also took active part in trying to broker a ceasefire between Iran and Iraq during their eight year war as a member of the United Nations Security Council and participating in the UNIIMOG mission which they became Acting Head of in the last few years before withdrawal. It later helped them to be elected into the OIC Peace Committee. Bangladesh strongly opposed the Israeli bombardment of South Lebanon which killed approximately 1,191 civilians and described it as "State Terrorism" and a double standard conflict going into detail that a non western nation would have been labelled a terrorist and a western nation would have never been deemed a terrorist. They also temporarily contributed to the peacekeeping effort after the 2006 Lebanon War by sending in battalions of infantry. Shortly after they were asked to leave as Bangladesh was not considered neutral by the UN Peacekeeping criteria such as refusing to recognise Israel.

With Republic of Iraq

Like many other nations in the Middle East, Iraq followed the same stance in supporting Pakistan during the Indo-Pakistan War of 1971 albeit they did so verbally and had not participated in transferring weapons to West Pakistan. After Bangladesh dispatched diplomats across the Middle East to explain their view of the conflict, Iraq became the first Arab nation to recognise Bangladesh in August 1972. Bangladesh and Iraq has missions located in Baghdad and Dhaka although Iraq closed theirs down after the Iraq War began but has expressed interest in reopening since last year. Bangladesh and Iraq's ties are primarily based on common faith but there hasn't been much progression into areas such as trade and investment. Between 1980 and 1986, Iraq sent five officers to study in Bangladesh's military academy in Dhaka. The only notable visit between the two nations was Saddam Hussein's visit to Bangladesh in 1988. The height of Bangladesh-Iraq relations was during the 1980s due to Bangladesh's role in trying to call for a ceasefire between Iraq and Iran during their war and was apart of UNIIMOG.

Relations quickly deterioated after Iraq invaded Kuwait sparking the Gulf War and a huge rise in oil prices. Bangladesh responded to the UN resolution demanding Iraq withdraw by the deadline or face military action. Bangladesh's other reasons for participation was because of the Bangladeshi community in Kuwait who some work on oil rigs and Kuwait is Bangladesh's oil supplier. Compared to Iraq's relation to its neighbours and the West, their relations with Bangladesh were considered satisfactory and this was displayed by deploying two engineer battalions rather than infantries to directly engage Iraqi troops. Relations would later improve after the US invasion of Iraq in 2003 when Bangladesh denied to send troops to Iraq despite America's persistance and stating that the UN should have had a primary role in solving the matter before the war. Currently they want a complete withdrawal from Iraq and has expressed support for reconstruction efforts.

With Iran

Although the nations are vastly different in culture and history, relations are very positive due to the majority population in both countries adhering to Islam. Another aspect of their relation is their fluctuating and unstable relationship with Pakistan and the concern over India's growing influence in the region. Immediately after the independence of Bangladesh, many non-Arab nations quickly recognised the new country. However, due to the strong pro-US attitude of the Shah and helping to transport weapons to West Pakistan during the Bangladesh Liberation War, relations did not occur until as late as 1979 after the Iranian Revolution which was greeted with unanimous support from Bangladeshis. Due to Ziaur Rahman's amendment in the constitution declaring to consolidate relations with Islamic states, relations have been progressive since and it has diverse into areas such as trade, investment and culture.

A turning point in relations was during the Iraq-Iran War when Bangladesh as a UN Security Council member tried to broker a ceasefire between the nations and settle their disputes with dialogue. Eventually, Bangladesh would participate in UNIIMOG mission to observe that agreements such as a ceasefire had been honoured. In 1995, Akbar Hashemi Rafsanjani became the first President of Iran to visit Bangladesh. The current president, Mahmoud Ahmadinejad is looking to strengthen relations with countries in South Asia such as Bangladesh by increasing Iranian investment like building oil refineries. In return, Bangladesh supports Iran to have full membership in the SAARC and its controversial nuclear program saying it is for "peaceful purposes".

In 2006, both countries signed a preferential trade accord which removes non-tariff barriers, hoping to take it further to a free trade agreement and in 2007, Bangladesh has requested Iranian assistance on building its nuclear power plant. Both countries are members of Developing 8 Countries, OIC, Like Minded Group and SAARC (although Iran has observer status). They have generally similar views on world issues especially on the occupation of Palestine.

With Israel

Israel is the only country in the world which is not recognised by Bangladesh. The latter has taken a similar stance with its fellow Muslim nations calling for the end to the Israeli occupation of Palestine and an independent Palestinian state. Bangladesh is also the only Muslim majority nation to have a complete ban on Israel even though this is a direct violation under the WTO protocols. As Bangladesh does not have any diplomatic relations with Israel it is illegal to travel there on a Bangladesh passport, as noted with the arrest of Salah Choudhury who is an editor of a tabloid called *The Weekly Blitz.* In the immediate aftermath of 2006 Lebanon War Bangladesh offered to send battalions of its infantrymen to help with the UN peacekeeping force, however Israel rejected it stating Bangladesh does not recognise Israel.

Although Israel rejected the country's participation, Bangladesh (and Nepal) were the first ones to reach the shores of South Lebanon whereas the western nations such as the original leader France delayed their deployment.

Immediately after setting ground for the other UN peacekeeping nations to work on, Bangladesh had to leave immediately as they were considered not to be neutral in the conflict based on the fact of refusing to recognise Israel and a comment made by Morshed Khan who described Israel's retaliation as double standard "State Terrorism".

With Kuwait

Relations between the two countries are considered strong based on common religion and values. A turning point in relations occurred during the Gulf War when Bangladesh sent a contingent of 2,300 personnel to monitor peace in Saudi Arabia and Kuwait and a contributor to UNIKOM with a mechanised infantry battalion. Bangladesh sends guests workers to Kuwait to enable its citizens to work in higher paying jobs leading to remittances as well as a Bangladeshi community in the country. Relations between the two countries have even indulged into military ties since the 1980s and a deal signed in February 1, 2004 under which Bangladesh Armed Forces are to provide technical and vocational training to the Kuwaiti army for the next six years.

Currently there is 4,000 Bangladeshi personnals operating in Kuwait. Relations have been strained due to the mistreatment of Bangladeshi workers such as harsh working conditions, low wages (or not being paid for weeks or even months) and several human rights breaches such as chaining or brutally beating workers.

There has been calls from the KSDD to replace the "sponsership system" with the ones used in western nations to avoid restrictions of freedom on foreign workers, who the head of the organisation described as a form of slavery.

With Lebanese Republic

Although culturally different, ties between the two are based on common background such as religious tolerance, the need to tackle Islamic militancy, similar views on global events and common religion. Bangladesh opposed Israel's bombing of South Lebanon during the 2006 Lebanon War and offered to contribute approximately 2,000 troops to the peacekeeping force. However, after establishing UN mission on the ground they were asked to leave for not meeting the UN criteria of neutrality such as the non-existent relations with Israel. Bangladesh like other South Asian countries also send workers to Lebanon to work in domestic and manual jobs, although many like those in the Gulf states complain of harsh conditions and low wages. During the 2006 Lebanon War, some of the Bangladeshis returned home but some went unpaid as their employers escaped the conflict by travelling abroad.

With Palestinian National Authority

Relations between Bangladesh and Palestine are considered to be warm and cordial as Bangladesh advocates for an independent Palestinian state and an end to Israeli occupation. Bangladesh is one of the 96 countries to recognise Palestine as a state since the Palestinian Declaration of Independence on November 15, 1988. There have been high level visits such as Yasir Arafat in 1981 and 1987 who was warmly received by both former presidents Ziaur Rahman and Hossain Mohammad Ershad with a favourable media. There is a wide public support for an independent Palestine as the Government had reported in 1987 that 8,000 had volunteered for the PLO although there had never been any official moves to send weapons or personnel. Since the 1980s, under IMET (International Military Education and Training) there have been development of military ties between the PLO and Bangladesh with the former attending one year courses at the Bangladesh Military Academy near Chittagong

With Kingdom of Saudi Arabia

From mid-1970s onward Bangladesh was seeking closer ties with oil rich Arab states such as Saudi Arabia. After the 1982 coup by Ershad, he visited Riyadh to meet with the King. Nine months later a ten member delegation of the Saudi military arrived in Bangladesh to discuss possible military ties and inspect its facilities. There was a rumour persisting amongst the press that the Saudis were considering to station a division of the Bangladesh army in the Kingdom (15,000 personnel). It was reported as a proposal by Ziaur Rahman although both governments deny this, the rumour continued into Ershad's rule. Since 1981, Saudi Arabia has sent 77 officers to the Defense Services Command & Staff College in Dhaka, which is the college's largest number of overseas graduates from a single nation. Bangladesh is seeking to increase economic ties with Saudi Arabia in order to reduce the trade deficit currently in the Kingdom's favour. One of their proposals is to export ceramics, leather and pharmaceutical products to the Kingdom as they are already doing with the western nations.

Australasia/Oceania

With Australia

Australia and Bangladesh enjoy good relations since Australia was the first western nation and the fourth in the world to recognise Bangladesh opening its embassy in Dhaka in 1972. There is also a Bangladeshi community present in the country.

With New Zealand

Relations between the two nations are friendly since

1971 with New Zealand amongst the few nations to quickly recognise Bangladesh. The trade balance between the two nations is satisfactory and remains in New Zealand's favour. Bangladesh exports its raw materials such as jute, textiles and clothing whereas New Zealand invests in areas such as banking, education and infrastructure development. There is also a small Bangladeshi community in New Zealand.

With European Union

Bangladesh's relations with the European Union and its member states remained a priority area in the foreign policy context. A number of achievements were made in the economic field during that brief period. At present EU is the top export destination of Bangladesh's products (48% of the total product). International Jute Study Group is being established in Dhaka. Bangladesh successfully participated in World Apparel Fair, European Seafood Exposition, Bangladesh Trade Show in Moscow and Kiev.

With French Republic

France and Bangladesh share an amicable relationship. In 1991, France cancelled Bangladesh's public debt (FRF 598M) as a gesture of goodwill. Trade between the two remains in Bangladesh's favour with France being its fourth biggest customer in 2005 (5.9% of Bangladeshi exports). France has many direct investments in the country such as the Lafarge cement plant in Chatak and has recently shown interest in aiding Bangladesh with the development of a nuclear power plant for civilian purposes.

With Federal Republic of Germany

After the independence of Bangladesh in 1971, Germany was one of the first European countries to officially recognise Bangladesh in 1972. Bangladesh also warmly greeted German reunification. As an economic power as well as an important member of the European Union (EU), Germany is a reliable partner of Bangladesh in development cooperation. Since independence German churches and numerous non-governmental organisations (NGOs) made tremendous efforts to promote the social and economic development of Bangladesh. German assistance to Bangladesh is received in the form of development efforts, trade and cultural cooperation. Both countries have a long and successful bilateral relationship on most international issues.

Germany always emphasises the democratic characteristics, governance issues and development process of Bangladesh. Germany developed as a democratic country in deep remorse for World War II and became one of the top most economic powers of the world. After establishment of diplomatic relations, the bilateral relations between the two countries began to grow steadily. Between the start of development cooperation in 1972 and the end of 2005, Bangladesh received approximately € 2.3 billion in commitments from Germany as part of bilateral financial and technical cooperation, in addition of the funds provided by the German churches and NGOs. At an intergovernmental negotiation in 2005, Bangladesh received € 14 million in new commitments from Germany. Since 1978, all German funds provided as part of government level cooperation have been in the form of non-repayable grants. Bangladesh is a priority partner country of German Development Cooperation (GTZ). By an agreement between both the government adopted in May 2004, the activities of the GTZ focus on three priority areas such as healthcare including family planning, economic reform and development of the market system through promotion of private sector, especially small and medium enterprises (SMEs), and renewable energies.

Among the other ongoing projects the promotion of legal and social empowerment of women in Bangladesh is also to be mentioned. The sustainable economic development programme of GTZ in Bangladesh contributes to the competitiveness of the readymade garments (RMG) sector, as well as other export-oriented sectors like silk, leather and jute. In trade with Germany, Bangladesh has for years recorded a large surplus. Germany is the second largest export market of Bangladesh after the US. Bangladesh exports in Germany in 2006 amounted to € 1.56 billion as compared with Bangladesh imports in the same period of only € 305 million. About 94% of the exports from Bangladesh to Germany are RMGs and Bangladesh imports mainly comprising machinery, chemical and electrical goods, and medicines.

A German-Bangladeshi investment promotion and protection agreement has been in force since 1986 and a bilateral double taxation accord since 1993. So far German direct investments in Bangladesh are almost € 60 million. The Bangladesh-German Chamber of Commerce and Industry (BGCCI) acts as a business platform and mediator between both the countries.

The cultural relationship of both the countries is very strong. The cultural cooperation between them is mainly channeled through the Goethe Institute that work on developing the cultural ties between both the countries by sponsoring local and German cultural activities. Bangladesh has traditional and historical connection with Germany. There is a century-old exchange between German and Bengali people. German interest in the culture of Bengal dates back to the visits to Germany by the Bengali national poet and Nobel laureate for literature Rabindranath Tagore in the 1920s and 1930s. Many Bangladeshi intellectuals take a keen and informed interest in German literature, art, architecture and philosophy. In Bangladesh Goethe Institute is the main meeting place for all those interested in Germany. Goethe-Institute Dhaka with headquarters in Munich offers a broad variety of cultural events to present the German culture in Bangladesh through its main activities by film-workshops, film-presentations, seminars and lectures on socio-political subjects as well as on aspects on contemporary arts, theatre performances, and exhibitions of German and Bangladeshi artists. Bangladesh has traditional and historical connection with Germany, and both the countries enjoy closest ties. There are increasing contracts amongst German and Bangladeshi artists, primarily in the fine arts, photography/film and theatre. Bangladeshi artists have been able to exhibit in German galleries and museums.

A number of visual artists from Bangladesh have also made Germany their new home. Germany continues to promote the restoration of historical monuments, archaeological research and the unique legacy of the Bengali catamarans. Since 1981, a cooperation agreement has been in place between Radio Bangladesh and Deutsche Welle (DW). The bilateral commercial and trade interests of both the countries are continuing, although there is considerable scope for greater engagement. Bilateral relations got some momentum by several high level visits, contracts, and political and economic dialogue. In December 2000, the then head of the government of Bangladesh officially visited Germany.

In February 2004, a German nine-member parliamentary delegation also visited Bangladesh. Both Germany and Bangladesh share common views on various international issues and work together in the UN and in other international forum. They have maintained and developed close and friendly relations in a wide range of field. The two countries are harmonized together by their commitment to various sectors mutually agreed upon, which is expected to be strengthened further in future.

With Kosovo

Both countries have suffered hardships and oppression by other ethnic groups who once lived in the same nation as them. Bengali people in East Pakistan suffered under a Punjabi dominated West Pakistan, as have Albanian majority Kosovo by a Serbian dominated central government. For reasons of differences and oppression of culture, race and enduring atrocities, both have sought for independence. Sunni Islam is a predominant religion in both countries and are generally secular and tolerant towards other religions (although Islam had been declared the state religion of Bangladesh and Islam isn't as influential in Kosovo's daily life). Due to these common grounds of tragic history, struggle for independence and religion, they are considered the extra initiatives for Bangladesh to recognise Kosovo. Bangladesh also sent its personnel to contribute towards the peacekeeping operations since the Kosovo crisis began and recently sent 120 policemen to the UN Kosovo mission.

Bangladesh originally declared that it will review the situation of Kosovo's independence and determine their actions afterwards. After a meeting between Fakhruddin Ahmed and James F. Moriarty, Bangladesh has shown intentions of recognising the new nation soon. On 29 June 2008 the Prime Minister, Fakhruddin Ahmed, during a meeting with the United States Ambassador to Bangladesh, James F. Moriarty, has affirmed that "Bangladesh will recognize the new European country". The Prime Minister also assured the US ambassador that "Bangladesh is committed to lobbying Asian Muslim countries to recognize

Kosovo. Bangladesh will actively contribute to the development of Kosovo".

With Russian Federation

Relations can be traced back to 1971 during the independence war when the Soviet Union sympathised with the Mukti Bahini cause and offered their assistance in the conflict. Although the start of their relations were very favourable, Bangladesh and Russia's relations have fluctuated greatly from extremely warm during the early 1970s to an all time low during the 1980s (attributed to the Soviet invasion of Afghanistan). After the collapse of the Soviet Union Bangladesh established ties with all the former Soviet Republics including Russia and began diversifying into other areas such as education, cultural, military and energy.

With Turkey

Relations have been excellent since Turkey recognised Bangladesh soon after independence. The trade volume between the two countries have grown as did Bangladeshi exports and has been in Bangladesh's favour throughout their economic relationship. Bangladesh was one of the only six countries to support the Turkish invasion of Cyprus during a UN vote on the matter. On the issue of Cyprus, Bangladesh at multilateral organisations such as the UN, use this as an opportunity to defend the rights of the Turkish minority.

With United Kingdom

The ties between Britain and Bangladesh date back to the British Raj. During the Bangladesh Liberation War Britain offered shelter to diplomats and people who escaped the conflict. The government, politicians and the media were also critical of the atrocities and shown empathy for the Mukti Bahini. On February 4th, 1972 Britain recognised Bangladesh, this eventually lead to recognition from other European and Commonwealth nations and Bangladesh's induction into the Commonwealth on April 18, 1972. Britain holds the largest Bangladeshi diaspora in the world, now numbered at around 500,000, most of them can trace their ties to the region of Sylhet. Britain also holds the largest open air Asian festival in Europe called Baishakhi Mela, a Bangladeshi event held in London.

There has been numerous delegation visits since Foreign Secretary Sir Alec Douglas-Home visited Bangladesh in June 1972. The first visit by a prime minister was James Callaghan in 1978. Other prime ministers who had visited Bangladesh are John Major in a 3-day visit between 10-12 January 1997 and Tony Blair in 2002. Presidents and Prime Ministers of Bangladesh such as Sheikh Mujib, Ziaur Rahman and Fakhruddin Ahmed have visted the UK. In March 2008, Fakhruddin Ahmed had visited Number 10 to discuss increasing British investment and cooperation in defence and trade, especially on counter-terrorism and duty-free access for LDCs. Britain is the largest foreign investor in Bangladesh and the third biggest export destination for Bangladeshi goods after USA and Germany. At the 7th ISS Asia Security Summit (also known as Shangri-La Dialogue) in Singapore, Bangladesh's Foreign advisor Iftekhar Ahmed Chowdhury met with UK's Defence Minister Des Browne at the sidelines to discuss security and defense relations between the two countries.

With Canada

Relations between the two countries are positive and there is approximately 100,000 Canadians of Bangladeshi origin living in Canada.

With United States of America

The United States is an aid donor to Bangladesh. It provides assistance during natural calamities. In the post 9/11 scenario, American policy-makers expressed support for moderation in one of the Muslim world's few democracies. The US State Department voiced support for free elections before 2008 ends. Approximately 150,000 citizens are of Bangladeshi origin with the majority in professional jobs. Before the 63rd UN General Assembly, Bangladesh's foreign minister had met with James F. Moriarty who is continuing his lobbying for Bangladesh's recognition of Kosovo and not to recognise the break-away regions of South Ossetia and Abkhazia. Iftekhar Ahmed Chowdhury has replied that Bangladesh will consider its national interests and decide what course of action they'll take.

With Brazil

Bangladesh's only embassy in South America is located in Brazil. Trade is the primary part of their relations exporting raw materials such as metals from its open mines and importing pharmaceutical products from Bangladesh.

Disputes - International

India

- 6.5 km of the border between India and Bangladesh remains to be demarcated.
- Dispute with Bangladesh over South Talpatti Island / New Moore in the Bay of Bengal.
- Ongoing discussions with Bangladesh to exchange 162 minuscule enclaves between the two.

REFERENCES

Bangladesh Foreign Acquisitions and Ties - Flags, Maps, Economy, History, Climate, Natural Resources, Current Issues, International Agreements, Population, Social Statistics....

Bangladesh police contingent to join UN peacekeeping in Kosovo - People's Daily Online.

"India fences off Bangladesh to keep out Muslim terror". Retrieved on 2007-07-11.

Religion in Bangladesh - Relations with the Islamic World.

Security concerns delay India-Bangladesh train link, Reuters, Jul 30, 2007.

The Tribune, Chandigarh, India - Main News.

8

Bhutan's External Affairs

Kingdom of Bhutan is a landlocked nation in South Asia, located at the eastern end of the Himalaya Mountains and is bordered to the south, east and west by the Republic of India and to the north by People's Republic of China. Bhutan is separated from Nepal by the Indian state of Sikkim. The Bhutanese call their country *Druk Yul* (Dzongkha which means "Land of the Thunder Dragon". Bhutan used to be one of the most isolated nations in the world, but developments including direct international flights, internet, mobile phone networks, and cable television have increasingly opened the doors. The population of Bhutan had been estimated based on the reported figure of about 1 million in the 1970s when the country had joined the United Nations and precise statistics were lacking. Thus using the annual increase rate of 2-3%, the most population estimates were around 2 million in the year 2000. A national census was carried out in 2005 and it turned out that the population was 672,425. Consequently, United Nations Population Division had down-estimated the country's population in the 2006 revision for the whole period from 1950 to 2050.

In 1971, sponsored by India, Bhutan began to develop its foreign relations by joining the UN, though it has no diplomatic relations with any of the permanent members on the UN Security Council. In 1981, Bhutan joined IMF and World Bank, followed by the World Health Organisation and UNESCO in 1982. It is also an active member of SAARC. Bhutan is currently a member of 45 international organisations.

BASIC FACTS	
Capital	Thimphu
Official languages	Dzongkha,English
Government	Constitutional monarchy
– King	Jigme Khesar Namgyel Wangchuck
– Prime Minister	Jigme Y. Thinley
Formation	Early 17th century
– Wangchuk Dynasty	17 December 1907
– Constitutional Monarchy	2008
Area	
– Total	47,000 km (131st) 18,147 sq mi
– Water (%)	<1 (estimate)
Population	
– estimate	672,425 (2005)
– Density	14/km
GDP (PPP)	2008 estimate
– Total	$3.442 billion
– Per capita	$5,238
HDI (2007)	0.579 (medium)
Currency	Ngultrum2 (BTN)
Time zone	BTT (UTC+6:00)

BILATERAL RELATIONS

With India

Historically, ties with India have been close. Both

countries signed a Friendship treaty in 1949, where India would assist Bhutan in foreign relations. On February 8, 2007, the Indo-Bhutan Friendship Treaty was substantially revised under the Bhutanese King, Jigme Khesar Namgyel Wangchuck. Whereas in the Treaty of 1949 Article 2 read as "The Government of India undertakes to exercise no interference in the internal administration of Bhutan. On its part the Government of Bhutan agrees to be guided by the advice of the Government of India in regard to its external relations." In the revised treaty it now reads as, "In keeping with the abiding ties of close friendship and cooperation between Bhutan and India, the Government of the Kingdom of Bhutan and the Government of the Republic of India shall cooperate closely with each other on issues relating to their national interests.

Neither government shall allow the use of its territory for activities harmful to the national security and interest of the other."

The revised treaty also includes in it the preamble "Reaffirming their respect for each other's independence, sovereignty and territorial integrity", an element that was absent in the earlier version. The Indo-Bhutan Friendship Treaty of 2007 strengthens Bhutan's status as an independent and sovereign nation.

With People's Republic of China

In fact, Bhutan has no diplomatic relations with its northern neighbour, the People's Republic of China. The border between Bhutan and China has been closed since invasion of Tibet in 1959, causing an influx of refugees. The border also remains undelineated; in 1961 China published a map that altered the traditional border. Tensions have since lessened, especially after the signing of a 1998 agreement on border peace and tranquility, the first bilateral agreement between China and Bhutan.

Despite the lack of formal diplomatic relations, Bhutan has also maintained an Honorary Consul in Macau since 2000 and Hong Kong since 2004. In late 2005, Bhutan claimed that Chinese soldiers were building roads and bridges within Bhutanese territory. Bhutanese Foreign Minister Khandu Wangchuk took up the matter with Chinese authorities after the issue was raised in Bhutanese parliament.

In response, Foreign Ministry spokesman Qin Gang of the People's Republic of China has said that the border remains in dispute and that the two sides continue to work for a peaceful and cordial resolution of the dispute; an Indian intelligence officer has also said that a Chinese delegation in Bhutan told the Bhutanese that they were overreacting. The Bhutanese newspaper *Kuensel* has said that China might use the roads to further Chinese claims along the border.

With Nepal

Since 1992, relations with Nepal have been tense due to the repatriation of refugees from Bhutan.

With Bangladesh

Along with India, Bangladesh is one of the only two nations to have a residential embassy in Bhutan. The relationship between Bhutan and Bangladesh have always been positive since 1971 when the former became the first country to recognise Bangladesh after gaining independence from Pakistan. Bhutan as well as Nepal see Bangladesh as another access to the sea and an opportunity to be less dependent on India and China.

Thus, so far Bhutan has diplomatic relations with 21 States. Gradually, it is making its presence in the comity of nation-states of the world. This tiny wonderland, though in fledgling state, may play important role in the new world order in coming days.

REFERENCES

"ADC Coordination offices". Austrian Development Agency.

"Bhutan Country Brief - August 2008". Department of Foreign Affairs and Trade.

"Bhutan's bilateral counterparts". Ministry of Foreign Affairs (Bhutan). Retrieved on 2008-08-06.

"Bhutan". Ministry for Foreign Affairs (Finland).

"Bhutan". Ministry of Foreign Affairs (Singapore).

"Canada-Bhutan Relations". Department of Foreign Affairs and International Trade.

"Country Profile : Bhutan". Foreign and Commonwealth Office.

"Embassy of India, Thimphu". Embassy of India in Thimphu.

"Embassy of the Kingdom of Bhutan". Ministry of Foreign Affairs (Netherlands).

"Embassy of the People's Republic of Bangladesh, Thimphu". Ministry of Foreign Affairs (Bangladesh).

"Embassy of the Republic of Singapore - Bhutan". Ministry of Foreign Affairs (Singapore).

"Heads of Missions". Department of Foreign Affairs and International Trade.

"Honorary consulates". Ministry of Foreign Affairs (Bhutan).

"Message from Ambassador". Ministry of Foreign Affairs (Denmark).

Ministry of Foreign Affairs (Bahrain) (29 May 2008). "Foreign Minister Receives a copy of Credentials of New Four Ambassadors". Press release.

Norbu, Ramphel et al., *Bhutan Through the Ages* (3 vols.), Anmol, New Delhi, 1999.

"Oslo Diplomatic List". Ministry of Foreign Affairs (Norway).

"The Stockholm Diplomatic List, June 2008". Ministry of Foreign Affairs (Sweden).

Wangchuk Karma, *Buddhism in Spiritual Lineage of Dzoychen Masters,* Anmol, New Delhi, 1998.

9

Sri Lankan Foreign Relations

Sri Lanka is an island country in South Asia, located about 31 kilometres (19.3 mi) off the southern coast of India. It is home to around twenty million people. Because of its location in the path of major sea routes, Sri Lanka is a strategic naval link between West Asia and South East Asia, and has been a center of Buddhist religion and culture from ancient times. Today, the country is a multi-religious and multi-ethnic nation, with more than a quarter of the population following faiths other than Buddhism, notably Hinduism, Christianity and Islam. The Sinhalese community forms the majority of the population, with Tamils, who are concentrated in the north and east of the island, forming the largest ethnic minority. Other communities include Moors, Burghers, Kaffirs and the Malays.

Famous for the production and export of tea, coffee, coconuts and rubber, Sri Lanka boasts a progressive and modern industrial economy and the highest per capita income in South Asia. The natural beauty of Sri Lanka's tropical forests, beaches and landscape, as well as its rich cultural heritage, make it a world famous tourist destination.

In case of foreign relations, generally, it is seen that Sri Lanka traditionally follows a nonaligned foreign policy but has been seeking closer relations with the United States since December 1977. It participates in multilateral diplomacy, particularly at the United Nations, where it seeks to promote sovereignty, independence, and development in the developing world. Sri Lanka was a founding member of the Non-Aligned Movement (NAM).

BASIC FACTS	
Capital	Sri Jayawardenapura-Kotte
Largest city	Colombo
Official languages	Sinhala, Tamil
Government	Democratic Socialist Republic
– President	Mahinda Rajapaksa
– Prime Minister	Ratnasiri Wickremanayake
Establishment	
– Foundation	543 BC
– Independence from the United Kingdom	February 4, 1948
– Republic	May 22, 1972
Area	
– Total	65,610 km2 (122nd) 25,332 sq mi
– Water (%)	4.4
Population	
– 2009 estimate	20,242,000 (52nd)
– July 2008 census	21,128,773
GDP (PPP)	2008 estimate
– Total	$92.018 billion
– Per capita	$4,581

It also is a member of the Commonwealth, the South Asian Association for Regional Cooperation (SAARC), the World Bank, International Monetary Fund, Asian Development Bank, and the Colombo Plan. Sri Lanka continues its active participation in the NAM, while also stressing the importance it places on regionalism by playing a strong role in SAARC.

Relations with India

The relation between India and Sri Lanka are generally friendly, but were controversially affected by the ongoing Sri Lankan civil war and by the failure of Indian intervention during the Sri Lankan civil war. India is the most important foreign player in Sri Lanka because India is the only neighbour of Sri Lanka.

With Pakistan

Sri Lanka has very close ties with Pakistan. Pakistan has been recently supplying military equipment to the Sri Lankan armed forces, especially during the era of former President Gen. Pervez Musharaff.. Though balmed internationally, as the harbour of Islamic terrorist onfits, Pakistan however is against and does not support the LTTE terrorists.

With Israel

Sri Lanka has a close relationship with Israel, and its military is a major user of Israeli weapons systems that include the IAI Kfir Fighter Jet, the Super Dvora Mk III class Patrol Vessel, and the Gabriel Missile

With Kosovo

Sri Lanka has declared that they will not recognise Kosovo as an independent state, and considers the unilateral declaration of independence to be a threat to world peace.

REFERENCE

"Sri Lanka says Kosovo independence a threat to world peace", AFP (2008-02-17). Retrieved on 17 February 2008.

10

International Relations of Maldives

The Maldives is the smallest Asian country in terms of both population and area; it is the smallest predominantly Muslim nation in the world. The Maldives or Maldive Islands, officially Republic of Maldives, is an island country in the Indian Ocean formed by a double chain of twenty-six atolls stretching in a north-south direction off India's Lakshadweep islands, between Minicoy Island and Chagos Archipelago. It stands in the Laccadive Sea, about seven hundred kilometres (435 mi) south-west of Sri Lanka in the Laccadive Sea of Indian Ocean. The twenty-six atolls of Maldives encompass a territory featuring 1,129 isletss, of which two hundered and fifty islands are inhabited.

The inhabitants were Buddhist, probably since Ashoka's period, in the 3rd centuryBC. Islam was introduced in 1153. The maldives then came under the influence of the Portugese (1558) and the Dutch (1654) seaborne empire. In 1887 it became a British protectorate. In 1965, the Maldives obtained independence from British (originally under the name "Maldive Islands") and in 1968 the Sultanate was replaced by a Republic.

It is remarkable to note that Maldives follows a non-aligned policy and has expressed its commitment to maintaining friendly relations with all countries.

BASIC FACTS	
Capital	Malé
Official languages	Dhivehi (Mahl)
Government	Presidential republic
– President	Mohamed Nasheed
Independent	
– from United Kingdom	26 July 1965
Area	
– Total	298 km^2 (206th)115 sq mi
– Water (%)	negligible
Population	
– 2009 estimate	309,000
– 2006 census	298,842
GDP (PPP)	2008 estimate
– Total	$1.713 billion
– Per capita	$4,967
GDP (nominal)	2008 estimate
– Total	$1.261 billion
– Per capita	$3,65
HDI (2007)	^{2}%0.771 (medium) (95th)
Currency	Maldivian Rufiyaa (MVR)

In fact, India enjoys a considerable influence over Maldives' foreign policy and provides extensive security co-operation especially after Operation Cactus in 1988 during which India repelled Tamil mercenaries who invaded the country. The maritime borders with India and Sri Lanka were demarcated through bilateral negotiations and agreements deposited with the UN Secretary General. The maritime border with the British Indian Ocean Territory (BIOT) remains undemarcated, with negotiations with the UK being broken off by the Maldives in the late 1990s. However, the Maldives has rejected offers by Mauritius to open negotiations on the demarcation of the maritime boundary between the Chagos Archipelago, which forms part of the BIOT. As founder member in 1985 of the South Asian Association for Regional Cooperation, SAARC, which brings together Afghanistan, Bangladesh, Bhutan, India, Maldives, Nepal, Pakistan and Sri Lanka, the country plays a very active role in SAARC.

The Maldives has taken the lead in calling for a South Asian Free Trade Agreement, the formulation of a Social Charter, the initiation of informal political consultations in SAARC forums, the lobbying for greater action on environmental issues, the proposal of numerous human rights measures such as the regional convention on child rights and for setting up a SAARC Human Rights Resource Centre. The Maldives is also an advocate of greater international profile for SAARC such as through formulating common positions at the UN.

Remarkably, Maldives also maintains close cultural relations with Islamic countries, and is a member of the Organisation of the Islamic Conference (OIC). However, the Maldives has often distanced itself from positions taken by the OIC on matters such as the Kashmir dispute, which it regards as a bilateral issue to be settled peacefully between India and Pakistan. It has also not supported the OIC position on issues such as that of Cyprus, subscribing to the stance taken by the UN.

In 1982, the Maldives joined the Commonwealth of Nations, first as special member and in 1985 became full member.

The Maldives has lately become a very strong advocate of human rights, as one of the earliest supporters of the Human Rights Council. For the past two years running, the Maldives was the only South Asian country to have voted against North Korea on human rights issues. In 2006, the Maldives acceded to the International Covenant on Civil and Political Rights, together with its optional protocol, as well as the International Convention on Economic, Social and Cultural Rights. In 2005, the Maldives became one of the promoters of the Optional Protocol to the UN Convention against Torture after having earlier acceded to the Convention against Torture. The Maldives is party to the Child Rights Convention, the Convention on the elimination of discrimination against women and its optional protocol.

In April 2006, the Maldives issued a standing invitation to all special procedures mandates of the UN human rights machinery to visit to the Maldives. While strongly supportive of the Palestinian cause, the Maldives had not, however, supported earlier calls for the expulsion of Israel from the UN, upholding its commitment to maintaining the universality of the UN. In 2005, the Maldives co-sponsored the resolution tabled by the USA on holocaust remembrance, and in 2007 it also co-sponsored the US-led resolution on condemning holocaust denial. In response to the Oslo peace process, the Maldives relaxed private sector restrictions on ties with Israel.

Further at the UN, the Maldives has highlighted the vulnerability of small states to various threats including terrorism, activities of mercenaries and organised crime. It is also a strong advocate of counter-terrorism and is party to all the main UN conventions against terrorism. Development co-operation is a major priority of the Maldives and it has been campaigning at the UN for a more structured means of graduation from the list of least developed countries targeted for preferential assistance.

The main donors to the Maldives are Japan, India, and Australia. The Maldives has a limited number of diplomatic missions. Denmark, Norway, the UK, Germany, Russian Federation, Italy, France, Netherlands, Turkey, and Sweden have consular agencies in Malé under the supervision of their embassies in Sri Lanka and India.

The UNDP has a representative resident in Malé, as do UNICEF and WHO. Many countries have nonresident ambassadors accredited to the Maldives, most of them based in Sri Lanka or India.

Appendix

COUNCIL ON FOREIGN RELATIONS

The Council on Foreign Relations (CFR) is an American nonprofit and nonpartisan membership organization dedicated to improving the understanding of U.S. foreign policy and international affairs. Founded in 1921 and headquartered at 58 East 68th Street (Park Avenue) in New York City, with an additional office in Washington, D.C., CFR is considered to be 'the most influential foreign-policy think tank.' It publishes a bi-monthly journal *Foreign Affairs*. It has an extensive website, www.cfr.org, featuring links to its history, fellows' biographical information, think tank, the David Rockefeller Studies Program, Independent Task Force reports and other reports, CFR books, expert interviews, meeting transcripts, audio, and videos, Emmy award-winning multimedia Crisis Guides and timelines, *Foreign Affairs*, and many other publications, biographies of notable directors and other board members, corporate members, and press releases.

Mission

As stated on its website, CFR's mission is to be "a resource for its members, government officials, business executives, journalists, educators and students, civic and religious leaders, and other interested citizens in order to help them better understand the world and the foreign policy choices facing the United States and other countries." CFR aims to maintain a diverse membership, including special programs to promote interest and develop expertise in the next generation of foreign policy leaders. It convenes meetings at which government officials, global leaders and prominent members of the foreign policy community discuss major international issues. Its think tank, the David Rockefeller Studies Program, is composed of about fifty adjunct and full-time scholars, as well as ten in-resident recipients of year-long fellowships, who cover the major regions and significant issues shaping today's international agenda. These scholars contribute to the foreign policy debate by making recommendations to the presidential administration, testifying before Congress, serving as a resource to the diplomatic community, interacting with the media, authoring books, reports, articles, and op-eds on foreign policy issues. CFR publishes *Foreign Affairs*, "the preeminent journal of international affairs and U.S. foreign policy." CFR also publishes Independent Task Forces which bring together experts with diverse backgrounds and expertise to work together to produce reports offering both findings and policy prescriptions on important foreign policy topics. To date, CFR has sponsored more than fifty reports.

CFR aims to provide up-to-date information and analysis about world events and U.S. foreign policy. In 2008, CFR.org's "Crisis Guide: Darfur" was awarded an Emmy Award by the Television Academy of Arts and Sciences, in the category of "New Approaches to News & Documentary Programming: Current News Coverage."

The earliest origin of the Council stemmed from a working fellowship of about 150 scholars, called "The Inquiry," tasked to brief President Woodrow Wilson about options for the postwar world when Germany was defeated. Through 1917–1918, this academic band, including Wilson's closest adviser and long-time friend "Colonel" Edward M. House, as well as Walter Lippmann, gathered at 155th Street and Broadway at the Harold Pratt House in New York City, to assemble the strategy for the postwar world. The team produced more than 2,000 documents detailing and analyzing the political, economic, and social facts globally that would be helpful for Wilson in the peace talks. Their reports formed the basis for the Fourteen Points, which outlined Wilson's strategy for peace after war's end.

These scholars then traveled to the Paris Peace Conference, 1919 that would end the war; it was at one of the meetings of a small group of British and American diplomats and scholars, on May 30, 1919, at the Hotel Majestic, that both the Council and its British counterpart, the Chatham House in London, were born.

Some of the participants at that meeting, apart from Edward House, were Paul Warburg, Herbert Hoover, Harold Temperley, Lionel Curtis, Lord Eustace Percy, Christian Herter, and American academic historians James Thomson Shotwell of Columbia University, Archibald Cary Coolidge of Harvard, and Charles Seymour of Yale.

In 1938 they created various Committees on Foreign Relations throughout the country. These later became governed by the American Committees on Foreign Relations in Washington, D.C.

About the Organization

The Council on Foreign Relations is a sister organization to the Institute of International Affairs, in London, was formed in 1922 as a noncommercial, nonpolitical organization supporting American foreign relations. From its inception the Council was bipartisan, welcoming members of both Democratic and Republican parties. It also welcomed Jews and African Americans, although women were initially barred from membership. Its proceedings were almost universally private and confidential. A study by two critics of the organization, Laurence Shoup and William Minter, found that of 502 government officials surveyed from 1945 to 1972, more than half were members of the Council.

Today it has about 5,000 members (including five-year term members between the ages of 35-40), which over its history have included senior serving politicians, more than a dozen Secretaries of State, former national security officers, bankers, lawyers, professors, former CIA members and senior media figures. As a private institution however, the CFR maintains through its official website that it is not a formal organization engaged in U.S. foreign policy-making, and its reports regularly take issue with U.S. government policy.

In 1962, the group began a program of bringing select Air Force officers to the Harold Pratt House to study alongside its scholars. The Army, Navy and Marine Corps requested they start similar programs for their own officers.

Vietnam created a rift within the organization. When Hamilton Fish Armstrong announced in 1970 that he would be leaving the helm of *Foreign Affairs* after 45 years, new chairman David Rockefeller approached a family friend, William Bundy, to take over the position. Anti-war advocates within the Council rose in protest against this appointment, claiming that Bundy's hawkish record in the State and Defense Departments and the CIA precluded him from taking over an independent journal. Some considered Bundy a war criminal for his prior actions.

Seven American presidents have addressed the Council, two while still in office – Bill Clinton and George W. Bush.

The Council says that it has never sought to serve as a receptacle for government policy papers that cannot be shared with the public, and they do not encourage government officials who are members to do so. The Council says that discussions at its headquarters remain confidential, not because they share or discuss secret information, but because the system allows members to test new ideas with other members.

Arthur M. Schlesinger, Jr., in his book on the Kennedy presidency, *A Thousand Days*, wrote that Kennedy was not part of what he called the "New York establishment":

"In particular, he was little acquainted with the New York financial and legal community— that arsenal of talent which had so long furnished a steady supply of always orthodox and often able people to Democratic as well as Republican administrations. This community was the heart of the American Establishment. Its household deities were Henry Stimson and Elihu Root; its present leaders, Robert Lovett and John J. McCloy; its front organizations, the Rockefeller, Ford and Carnegie foundations and the Council on Foreign Relations; its organs, the *New York Times* and *Foreign Affairs*."

Influence on Foreign Policy

Beginning in 1939 and lasting for five years, the Council achieved much greater prominence with government and the State Department when it established the strictly confidential *War and Peace Studies*, funded entirely by the Rockefeller Foundation. The secrecy surrounding this group was such that the Council members (total at the time: 663) who were not involved in its deliberations were completely unaware of the study group's existence.

It was divided into four functional topic groups: economic

and financial, security and armaments, territorial, and political. The security and armaments group was headed by Allen Welsh Dulles who later became a pivotal figure in the CIA's predecessor, the OSS. It ultimately produced 682 memoranda for the State Department, marked classified and circulated among the appropriate government departments. As a historical judgment, its overall influence on actual government planning at the time is still said to remain unclear.

In an anonymous piece called "The Sources of Soviet Conduct" that appeared in *Foreign Affairs* in 1947, CFR study group member George Kennan coined the term "containment." The essay would prove to be highly influential in US foreign policy for seven upcoming presidential administrations. 40 years later, Kennan explained that he had never meant to contain the Soviet Union because it might be able to physically attack the United States; he thought that was obvious enough that he didn't need to explain it in his essay. William Bundy credited the CFR's study groups with helping to lay the framework of thinking that led to the Marshall Plan and NATO. Due to new interest in the group, membership grew towards 1,000.

Dwight D. Eisenhower chaired a CFR study group while he served as President of Columbia University. One member later said, "whatever General Eisenhower knows about economics, he has learned at the study group meetings." The CFR study group devised an expanded study group called "Americans for Eisenhower" to increase his chances for the presidency. Eisenhower would later draw many Cabinet members from CFR ranks and become a CFR member himself. His primary CFR appointment was Secretary of State John Foster Dulles. Dulles gave a public address at the Harold Pratt House in which he announced a new direction for Eisenhower's foreign policy: "There is no local defense which alone will contain the mighty land power of the communist world. Local defenses must be reinforced by the further deterrent of massive retaliatory power." After this speech, the council convened a session on "Nuclear Weapons and Foreign Policy" and chose Henry Kissinger to head it. Kissinger spent the following academic year working on the project at Council headquarters. The book of the same name that he published from his research in 1957 gave him national recognition, topping the national bestseller lists.

On 24 November 1953, a study group heard a report from political scientist William Henderson regarding the ongoing conflict between France and Vietnamese Communist leader Ho Chi Minh's Viet Minh forces, a struggle that would later become known as the First Indochina War. Henderson argued that Ho's cause was primarily nationalist in nature and that Marxism had "little to do with the current revolution." Further, the report said, the United States could work with Ho to guide his movement away from Communism. State Department officials, however, expressed skepticism about direct American intervention in Vietnam and the idea was tabled. Over the next twenty years, the United States would find itself allied with anti-Communist South Vietnam and against Ho and his supporters in Vietnam War.

The Council served as a "breeding ground" for important American policies such as mutual deterrence, arms control, and nuclear non-proliferation.

A four-year long study of relations between America and China was conducted by the Council between 1964 and 1968. One study published in 1966 concluded that American citizens were more open to talks with China than their elected leaders. Kissinger had continued to publish in *Foreign Affairs* and was appointed by President Nixon to serve as National Security Adviser in 1969. In 1971, he embarked on a secret trip to Beijing to broach talks with Chinese leaders. Nixon went to China in 1972, and diplomatic relations were completely normalized by President Carter's Secretary of State, another Council member, Cyrus Vance.

In November 1979, while chairman of the CFR, David Rockefeller became embroiled in an international incident when he and Henry Kissinger, along with John J. McCloy and Rockefeller aides, persuaded President Jimmy Carter through the State Department to admit the Shah of Iran, Mohammad Reza Pahlavi, into the US for hospital treatment for lymphoma. This action directly precipitated what is known as the Iran hostage crisis and placed Rockefeller under intense media scrutiny (particularly from *The New York Times*) for the first time in his public life.

World Order in the 21st Century

The CFR started a program in 2008 to last for 5 years called "International Institutions and Global Governance: World Order in the 21st Century" which aims in setting up global institutions in different levels to foster a global governance, in order to tackle different trans-national problems.

(a) Countering Transnational Threats, including terrorism, proliferation of WMD, and infectious disease.

(b) Protecting the Environment and Promoting Energy Security.

(c) Managing the Global Economy.

(d) Preventing and Responding to Violent Conflict.

In August 2009, the Obama Administration urged cooperation with UN to tackle the same points covered by CFR plan's. "The Obama administration will work with the United Nations to fight terrorism and other major world challenges...like nuclear programs of Iran and North Korea, the global financial crisis, wars in Afghanistan and Iraq, pandemics and global warming."

Membership

There are two types of membership: life, and term membership, which lasts for 5 years and is available to those between 30 and 36. Only U.S. citizens (native born or naturalised) and permanent residents who have applied for U.S. citizenship are eligible. A candidate for life membership must be nominated in writing by one Council member and seconded by a minimum of three others.

Corporate membership (250 in total) is divided into "Basic", "Premium" ($25,000+) and "President's Circle" ($50,000+). All corporate executive members have opportunities to hear distinguished speakers, such as overseas presidents and prime ministers, chairmen and CEOs of multinational corporations, and U.S. officials and Congressmen. President and premium members are also entitled to other benefits, including attendance at small, private dinners or receptions with senior American officials and world leaders.

BOARD OF DIRECTORS

Office	*Name*
Co-Chairman of the Board	Carla A. Hills
Co-Chairman of the Board	Robert E. Rubin
Vice Chairman	Richard E. Salomon
President	Richard N. Haass

Board of Directors	
Director	Peter Ackerman
Director	Fouad Ajami
Director	Madeleine Albright
Director	Charlene Barshefsky
Director	Henry Bienen
Director	Alan Blinder
Director	Stephen W. Bosworth
Director	Tom Brokaw
Director	Sylvia Mathews Burwell
Director	Frank J. Caufield
Director	Kenneth Duberstein
Director	Richard N. Foster
Director	Stephen Friedman
Director	Ann M. Fudge
Director	Maurice R. Greenberg
Director	J. Tomilson Hill
Director	Richard Holbrooke
Director	Alberto Ibargüen
Director	Shirley Ann Jackson
Director	Henry Kravis
Director	Jami Miscik
Director	Joseph Nye
Director	Ronald L. Olson
Director	James W. Owens
Director	Colin Powell
Director	David Rubenstein
Director	George E. Rupp
Director	Anne-Marie Slaughter
Director	Joan E. Spero
Director	Vin Weber
Director	Christine Todd Whitman
Director	Fareed Zakaria

The Board of Directors of the Council on Foreign Relations is composed in total of thirty-six officer's. Peter G. Peterson and David Rockefeller are Directors Emeriti (Chairman Emeritus and Honorary Chairman, respectively). It also has an International Advisory Board consisting of thirty-five distinguished individuals from across the world.

Corporate Members

The following members are listed on the Corporate Roster of the Council on Foreign Relations:

- AARP
- Access Industries, Inc.
- ACE Limited
- AEA Investors Inc.
- Airbus North America
- Alcoa, Inc.
- Allied World Assurance Company, Ltd.
- American Express Company
- Apollo Management, LP
- ARAMARK Corporation
- Aramco Services Company
- Archer Daniels Midland Company
- AREVA Inc.
- Arnhold and S. Bleichroeder Holdings, Inc.
- Arnold & Porter LLP
- Baker & Hostetler LLP
- Baker Capital Corp.
- Baker, Nye Advisers, Inc.
- Baldwin-Gottschalk Group, The

- Banca d'Italia
- Banco Mercantil
- Bank of America / Merrill Lynch & Co., Inc.
- Bank of New York Mellon Corporation, The
- Barclays Capital
- BASF Corporation
- Bennett Jones LLP
- BGR International
- Blackstone Group L.P., The
- Bloomberg
- BNP Paribas
- Boeing Company, The
- Booz & Co.
- Booz Allen Hamilton Inc.
- BP p.l.c.
- Bridgewater Associates, Inc.
- Bunge Limited
- CA
- CALYON Corporate and Investment Bank
- Canadian Imperial Bank of Commerce
- Canon, Inc.
- Caxton Associates
- Chevron Corporation
- Chrysler LLC
- Cisneros Group of Companies
- CIT Group Inc.
- Citi

- Clarium Capital Management, LLC
- Cleary Gottlieb Steen & Hamilton LLP
- CNA Corporation, The
- Coca-Cola Company, The
- ConocoPhillips Company
- Continental Properties
- Control Risks Group
- Corsair Capital
- Covington & Burling
- Craig Drill Capital Corporation
- Credit Suisse
- De Beers
- Debevoise & Plimpton LLP
- Deere & Company
- Deloitte
- Deutsche Bank AG
- Duke Energy Corporation
- DynCorp International
- Energy Intelligence Group, Inc.
- Eni S.p.A.
- Equinox Partners, L.P.
- Estee Lauder Companies Inc.
- Exxon Mobil Corporation
- Federal Express Corporation
- Ford Motor Company
- Fortress Investment Group LLC
- Freeport-McMoRan Copper and Gold Inc.

- French-American Chamber of Commerce
- Future Pipe Industries, Inc.
- General Atlantic LLC
- General Electric Company
- Gibson Dunn & Crutcher, LLP
- GlaxoSmithKline
- Goldman Sachs Group, Inc.
- Google, Inc.
- Granite Associates LP
- Greenberg Traurig, LLP
- Guardsmark LLC
- Hemispheric Partners
- Hess Corporation
- Hitachi, Ltd.
- IBM Corporation
- Idemitsu Apollo Corporation
- Indus Capital Partners, LLC
- Intellispace, Inc.
- Intesa Sanpaolo
- Investcorp International, Inc.
- Invus Group, LLC
- ITOCHU International
- J.E. Robert Companies
- Jacobs Asset Management, LLC
- Japan Bank for International Cooperation
- JETRO New York
- Joukowsky Family Foundation

- JPMorgan Chase & Co
- Kailix Investment Advisors
- KBR
- Kingdon Capital Management
- Kohlberg Kravis Roberts & Co.
- Kometal GMBH Austria
- Korn/Ferry International
- Kuwait Petroleum Corporation
- Lazard
- Lockheed Martin Corporation
- MacAndrews & Forbes Holdings Inc.
- Mannheim LLC
- Marathon Oil Company
- Mark Partners
- Mars, Inc.
- Marsh & McLennan Companies, Inc.
- Marubeni America Corporation
- MBIA Insurance Corporation
- McGraw-Hill Companies, The
- McKinsey & Company, Inc.
- MeadWestvaco Corporation
- Medley Capital
- Medley Global Advisors
- Merck & Co., Inc.
- Milbank, Tweed, Hadley & McCloy LLP
- Mitsubishi Heavy Industries America, Inc.
- Mitsubishi International Corporation

- Mitsui USA Foundation
- Moody's Investors Service
- Moore Capital Management LLC
- Morgan Stanley
- Morgan, Lewis & Bockius LLP
- Munich Re America Corporation
- National Interest Security Company
- New Media Investments
- New York Life International, Inc.
- News Corporation, The
- Nike, Inc.
- NYSE Euronext
- Occidental Petroleum Corporation
- Olayan Group, The
- Oxford Analytica Inc.
- PepsiCo, Inc.
- Pfizer Inc.
- Pillsbury Winthrop Shaw Pittman LLP
- PricewaterhouseCoopers LLP
- Principal Financial Group
- Prudential Life Insurance Co.
- Raytheon Company
- Reliance Industries Limited
- Resource Holdings, Ltd.
- Rho Capital Partners
- Rio Tinto
- Rockefeller Group International, Inc.

- Rohatyn Group, The
- Rothschild North America, Inc.
- Shell Oil Company
- Silver Lake Partners
- Simpson Thacher & Bartlett LLP
- Sony Corporation of America
- Soros Fund Management
- Standard & Poor's
- Standard Chartered Bank
- Starwood Capital Group
- Strategic Real Estate Advisors
- Sullivan & Cromwell LLP
- Tata Group, The
- The Nasdaq OMX Group
- Thomson Reuters
- Time Warner Inc.
- Tishman Speyer Properties, Inc.
- TOTAL S.A.
- Toyota Motor North America, Inc.
- Turkish Industrialists' and Businessmen's Association
- U.S. Chamber of Commerce
- UBS AG
- United Technologies Corporation
- Veritas Capital LLC
- Verizon Communications Inc.
- Visa Inc.
- Volkswagen of America, Inc.

- Vornado Realty Trust
- Warburg Pincus LLC
- Weber Shandwick Worldwide
- Weiss Multi-Strategy Advisors, LLC
- Wyoming Investment Corporation
- Xerox Corporation
- Zephyr Management, L.P.
- Ziff Brothers Investments LLC

Notable Historical Members

- Kenneth Bacon
- Conrad Black (International Advisory Board member)
- McGeorge Bundy
- William Bundy
- C. Douglas Dillon
- Allen Dulles
- John Foster Dulles
- President Gerald Ford
- Sergei Karaganov (International Advisory Board member)
- George Kennan
- Robert Lovett
- John J. McCloy
- Charles Peter McColough
- Robert McNamara
- Paul Nitze
- Nelson Rockefeller

- John D. Rockefeller 3rd
- Felix Rohatyn
- Mark B. Rosenberg
- Eugene Rostow
- Walt Rostow
- Dean Rusk
- Arthur Schlesinger
- Strobe Talbott
- Albert Wohlstetter
- Roberta Wohlstetter
- Paul Warburg
- Caspar Weinberger

[***Source:*** Wikipedia]

Glossary

Accession: The procedure by which a nation becomes a party to an agreement already in force between other nations

Accords: International agreements originally thought to be for lesser subjects than covered by treaties , but now really treaties by a different name.

Ad Referendum: An agreement reached ad referendum means an agreement reached by negotiators at the table, subject to the subsequent concurrence of their governments.

Agrément: Diplomatic courtesy requires that before a state appoints a new chief of diplomatic mission to represent it in another state, it must be first ascertained whether the proposed appointee is acceptable to the receiving state. The acquiescence of the receiving state is signified by its granting its agrément to the appointment. It is unusual for an agrément to be refused, but it occasionally happens.

Aide Mémoire: A written summary of the key points made by a diplomat in an official conversation. Literally, a document left with the other party to the conversation, either at the time of the conversation or subsequently, as an aid to memory.

Alternat: When an agreement is signed between two states, or among several states, each signatory keeps an official copy for itself. Alternat refers to the principle which provides that a state's own name will be listed ahead of the other signatory, or signatories, in its own official copy. It is a practice devised centuries ago to handle sensitivities over precedence.

Ambassador Extraordinary and Plenipotentiary: The chief of a diplomatic mission; the ranking official diplomatic representative of his country to the country to which he is accredited, and the personal representative of his own head of state to the head of state of the host country. The term "extraordinary" has no real meaning. Years ago it was given only to nonresident ambassadors on temporary missions and was used to distinguish them from regular resident ambassadors. The latter resented others having this appellation, as it seemed to imply a lesser position for themselves. Eventually therefore, it was accorded to them as well. "Plenipotentiary" also comes down through the years. Today it simply means possessed of full power to do an ambassador's normal job. Ambassador is capitalized when referring to a specific person (i.e. Ambassador Smith).

Ambassador-Designate: An official who has been named to be an ambassador, but who has not yet taken his oath of office.

Ambassadress: A term often used to denote the wife of an ambassador, and misused to denote a woman chief of mission. The latter is an ambassador, not an ambassadress.

Asylum: Used in diplomacy to mean the giving of refuge in two senses: first, within the extraterritorial grounds of an embassy (not generally done in American embassies); and second, when one states allows someone to live within its borders, out of reach of the authority of a second state from which the person seeks protection.

Attaché: Civilian attachés are either junior officers in an embassy or, if more senior, officers who have a professional specialization such as "labor attaché", "commercial attaché", "cultural attaché", etc. On the military side, an embassy will generally have either an army attaché, naval attaché, or air attaché – and often all three. In American embassies, the senior of the three is called the defense attaché and is in charge of all military attaché activities. These consist largely of liaison work with local military authorities and of keeping informed on host country order of battle.

Bag, The: See "Pouch". Bag is the British term. "Bag Day" is the day the pouch is sealed and sent to the home office. Hence, bag day is the day when all non-telegraphic reporting must be finalized and dispatched.

Belligerency: A state of belligerency is a state of armed conflict. Belligerents are direct participants in the conflict.

Bilateral: Bilateral discussions or negotiations are between a state and one other. A bilateral treaty is between one state and one other. "Multilateral" is used when more than two states are involved.

Bout de Papier: A very informal means of conveying written information; more informal than an aide mémoire or a memorandum.

Breaking Relations: The formal act of severing diplomatic relations with another state to underscore disapproval of its actions or policies. It is generally an unwise step, because when relations between states are most strained is when the maintaining of diplomatic relations is most important. It makes little sense to keep diplomats on the scene when things are going relatively well and then take them away when they are most needed. An intermediate step which indicates serious displeasure but stops short of an actual diplomatic break is for a government to recall its ambassador indefinitely. This is preferable to a break in relations as his embassy will continue to function; but again this comes under the heading of cutting one's nose to spite one's face. If a dramatic gesture of this kind is needed, it is far better promptly and publicly to recall an ambassador for consultations, and then just as promptly return him to his post.

Calls and Calling Cards: "Calling" has largely disappeared from private life, but it is a practice which is still useful in a diplomatic community where the early establishment of extensive contacts is a must. Soon after a diplomat's arrival at a new post, therefore, he will embark on a program of call on those with whom he will be dealing – and whom he must lose no time in getting to know. In modern, less formal times, calling cards do not have nearly the same role in diplomatic life they once did. But with the traditional initials, p.p. (pour présenter); p.f. (pour féliciter); p.c. (pour condoléance); p.r. (pour remercier); or p.p.c. (pour prendre congé) inscribed at their bottom left-hand corner, they remain a still useful and accepted way to convey simple messages of presentation, congratulation, condolence, thanks, and farewell.

Casus Belli: An action by one state regarded as so contrary to the interests of another state as to be considered by that second state as a cause for war.

Chancelleries: As in "chancelleries of Europe," i.e. foreign offices.

Chancery: The office where the chief of mission and his staff work. This office is often called the embassy but this is a misnomer. Technically, the embassy is where the ambassador lives, not where he works, although in earlier times when diplomatic missions were smaller, this was usually the same building. Today, for clarity's sake, many diplomats now distinguish between the two by using the terms "embassy residence" and "embassy office".

Chancery, Head of: An important position in British embassies not found in American diplomatic establishments. An officer, usually head of the political section, charged with coordinating the substantive and administrative performance of the embassy. In an American embassy, the ambassador looks to the deputy chief of mission to do this.

Chief of Mission: The ranking officer in an embassy, permanent mission, legation, consulate general or consulate (i.e. an ambassador always, and a minister, consul general, or consul when no more senior officer is assigned to the post). A "chief of mission" can also be the head of a special and temporary diplomatic mission, but the term is usually reserved for the earlier listed examples.

Clearances: A message or other document conveying a policy or an instruction is "cleared" in a foreign office, or large embassy, when all officials who have responsibility for any of its specific aspects have signified their approval by initialing it. Some officers gain a reputation for insisting on changing, even if only in minor ways, everything that is places before them – and it is occasionally alleged they would do so even if it were in the Ten Commandments being presented to them. Conversely, others are occasionally so casual that their clearance seems to mean only that the document in question does not appear to take away any of their jurisdiction. A clearance procedure in some form is essential for adequate coordination, but when overdone (as it often is), it can be a stifling, time-consuming process, and a bane of diplomatic life.

Conciliation: An effort to achieve agreement and, hopefully, increased goodwill between two opposed parties.

Concordat: A treaty to which the Pope is a party.

Conference or Congress: International meetings. In the diplomatic sense, a congress has the same meaning as a conference.

Consular Agent: An official doing consular work for a nation in a locality where it does not maintain a regular consulate. This official is usually a national of his host state, and his work is usually part-time.

Consulate: An office established by one state in an important city of another state for the purpose of supporting and protecting its citizens traveling or residing there. In addition, these offices are charges with performing other important administrative duties such as issuing visas (where this is required) to host country nationals wishing to travel to the country the consulate represents. All consulates, whether located in the capital city or in other communities, are administratively under the ambassador and the embassy. In addition to carrying out their consular duties, they often serve as branch offices for the embassy, supporting, for example, the latter's political and economic responsibilities. Consulates are expected to play a particularly significant role in connection with the promotion of their own country's exports and other commercial activities. Officers performing consular duties are known as consuls or, if more junior, vice consuls. The chief of the consulate is known as the consul.

Consulate General: A bigger and more important consulate, presided over by a consul-general.

Consul, Honorary: A host-country national appointed by a foreign state to perform limited consular functions in a locality here the appointing state has no other consular representation.

Convention: An agreement between two or more states, often more, concerning matters of common interest. While supposedly used for lesser matters than embraced in a treaty, it often deals with important subjects indeed – international postal and copyright laws, for example, of the law of the sea.

Counselor of Embassy: A senior diplomatic title ranking just behind an ambassador and a minister. In many embassies there is no minister, and the counselor is the number two man, i.e., the deputy chief of mission. (In a very small embassy, the second may not have this rank). In a large embassy, the second ranking officer may be a minister, or minister-counselor, in which case the heads of the more important sections have counselor rank. Thus, for example, the embassy's political counselor, economic counselor, an administrative counselor are well-known and much-respected positions in diplomatic life.

Country Desk: State departments and foreign offices generally have an office for each country with which the have active dealings. These offices are often called country desks, and if a large country is involves and there is a large embassy to support there, the desk is likely to be staffed by a large number of officers. A smaller country may require a one-officer desk only.

Country Team: An American diplomatic term meaning the ambassador's cabinet. It consists of his deputy chief of mission, heads of all important embassy sections, and the chiefs of all other elements (military, agricultural, aid, information, and cultural, etc.) working under him in the "embassy community".

Credentials: The name for letters given to an ambassador by his chief of state, and addressed to the chief of state of his host country. They are delivered to the latter by ambassadors in a formal credentials ceremony, which generally takes place shortly after his arrival at a new post. Until this ceremony has taken place he is not formally recognized by the host country, and he cannot officially act as an ambassador. The letters are termed "letters of credence" because they request the receiving chief of state to give "full credence" to what the ambassador will say of behalf of his government.

D.C.M.: Embassy shorthand for the deputy chief of mission.

Declaration: This can have two quite distinct meanings in diplomacy. It can first, of course, mean a unilateral statement by one state, ranging from an expression of opinion or policy to a declaration of war. It can also mean a joint statement by two or more states having the same binding effect as a treaty. In this latter connection declarations can be put forward either in their own right or appended to a treaty as an added understanding or interpretation.

Delegation: Again used in two senses in diplomacy. "Delegation" can be the term used to refer to the specific powers delegates by his government to a diplomat acting in certain specific circumstances. It also refers to an official party sent to an international conference or on some other special diplomatic mission.

Demarché: An approach, a making of representations. Still very common term used by diplomats to indicate the official raising of a matter with host country officials, often accompanied by a specific request for some type of action or decision in connection with it.

Détente: An easing of tension between states.

Diplomatic Agent: A generic term denoting a person who carries out regular diplomatic relations of the nation he/she represents in the nation to which he/she has been accredited.

Diplomatic Corps: The body of foreign diplomats assembled at a nation's capital. In cities where consuls and consul general are resident, the are collectively known as the consular corps. The dean of both corps is usually that official who had been at his post the longest. There are exceptions to this later rule, however. For example, in some Catholic countries, the papal nuncio is always the dean. The dean represents the corps in collective dealings with host country officials on matters of a ceremonial or administrative character affecting the corps as a whole.

Diplomatic Illness: The practice of feigning illness to avoid participation in a diplomatic event of one kind or another and at the same time to avoid giving formal offense. "Diplomatic deafness" is a somewhat related concept whereby older diplomats allegedly turn this infirmity to advantage by not hearing what they prefer not to hear.

Diplomatic Immunity: Exemption of foreign diplomatic agents or representatives from local jurisdiction. Also see Diplomatic Immunity.

Diplomatic Note: A formal written means of communication among embassies.

Diplomatic Privileges and Immunities: Historically accorded in recognition that the diplomat represents (and is responsible to) a different sovereignty; also in order that the legitimate pursuit of his official duties will not be impeded in any unnecessary way. They include inviolability of person and premises and exemption from taxation and the civil and criminal jurisdiction of local courts. Also see Diplomatic Immunity.

Diplomatist: It has the same meaning as "diplomat". An outdated word rarely used now in spoken diplomacy but occasionally still appearing in the literature of diplomacy.

Dispatch: A written, as opposed to a telegraphic, message from an embassy to its home office or vice versa.

Dual Accreditation: Having two or more responsibilities, such as an ambassador who is simultaneously accredited to two nations.

Economic Officer: A career diplomat who specialized in economics rather than political, administrative, or other matters.

Embassy: The residence of an ambassador. In recent years, also inaccurately used to denote the building which contains the offices of the ambassador and other key members of his staff. The proper term for the latter, as noted above, is the "chancery". As also noted above, confusion is nowadays avoided through the practice of using the two terms "embassy residence" and "embassy office".

Entente: Denotes a close understanding between certain nations. It suggests mutual and complementary efforts, and a sense of compatible objectives. It can be agreed on orally or in writing, but as a concept is generally less binding than a treaty relationship.

Envoy: Nowadays used to refer to any senior diplomat. Earlier it had a specific hierarchical connotation, being used to designate diplomatic agents of less than the highest rank.

Excellency: An archaic but still much-used title for addressing an ambassador. Theoretically, an American ambassador is not supposed to be addressed this way, but he generally is – along with all his other ambassadorial colleagues. "Mr. Ambassador" is more accurate and less silly. That he is; he may or may not be "excellent."

Exchange of Notes: A common way of recording an agreement. The contents of the notes are, of course, agreed upon in advance by the two nations participating in the exchange.

Exequatur: A document issued to a consul by the host

country government authorizing him to carry out his consular duties.

Ex Gracia: Something which is done as a gesture of good will and not on the basis of an accepted legal obligation.

Extradition: The term for the process, governed by formally concluded agreements, by which fugitives fleeing justice from one country are returned from the country where they have sought refuge. It does not apply to political offenses.

Extraterritoriality: The exercise by one nation, as a result of formally concluded agreements, of certain sovereign functions within the territory of another state. A curtailment of the jurisdiction of the latter state in certain specified areas and/or in certain specified respects.

Final Act (Acte Final): A formal summary statement, drawn up at the conclusion of a conference.

Foggy Bottom: The name given to a once marsh like area near Washington's Potomac River, and now somewhat irreverently bequeathed to the U.S. Department of State, one of that area's best-known modern occupants.

Foreign Affairs Community: An American government term used to denote the State Department and other government departments and agencies (Defense, Commerce, Agriculture, Treasury, U.S. Information Agency, the Central Intelligence Agency, the Agency for International Development, etc.) which have special interests and responsibilities in the foreign affairs field.

F.S.O.: Shorthand for a career American diplomat, i.e., an American Foreign Service officer.

Full Powers: A document which authorizes a diplomat to conduct and consummate special business on behalf of his government, such as the settlement of a dispute or the negotiation and signing of a treaty. Before signing a treaty, a diplomat is obligated to show his full-powers document to the other parties involved.

Good Offices: An effort by a third state, or by an individual or an international body, designed to stimulate the processes of settlement in a dispute between two other states.

Guarantee, Treaty of: A treaty which requires signatories to guarantee that situations agreed upon will be maintained. The honoring of such commitments can precipitate armed conflicts.

High Commission: A diplomatic mission of one Commonwealth country in another. For example, Canada has a High Commission in Canberra, Australia.

High Commissioner: The chief of a high commission. Similar to what an ambassador is to an embassy.

Legation: These are rare now, but they were once very common. A legation is a diplomatic mission similar for most practical purposes to an embassy, but lower in rank, and presided over by a minister rather than an ambassador. For most of the last century, American diplomatic representation abroad was limited to legations, and for much of this century, the U.S. was represented in more countries by legations than it was by embassies.

Letters of Recall: Also presented by a new ambassador, along with his letter of credence, to the chief of state of his host country during his credentials-presentation ceremony. It is the official document which formally recalls his predecessor.

Minister, Minister-Counselor: Apart from its cabinet-officer connotation (i.e. "foreign minister"), a minister has traditionally been a chief of diplomatic mission who headed a legation rather than an embassy. As so few legations are left, the title is now borrowed more and more to designate the second-ranking officer of a large embassy. It has, therefore, come increasingly to mean the senior counselor under the ambassador. To avoid confusion with the old connotation, the United States and a number of governments designate these senior deputy chiefs of mission by the hyphenated title "minister-counselor".

Mission: A generic term for embassy. Mission also describes the entirety of official representation in a given foreign country which functions under the supervision of the Ambassador, including civilian and military personnel.

Modus Vivendi: A temporary agreement, in writing, of an interim character, pending the negotiation of more definitive arrangements.

Passport: The official document issued to a person by his/her government certifying citizenship and requesting foreign governments to grant the individual safe passage, lawful aid and protection while under that government's jurisdiction.

P.C.: Used in written social correspondence, "pour condoler" (to express sympathy).

P.F.: Used in written social correspondence, "pour féliciter" (to extend congratulations).

P.M.: Used in written social correspondence, "pour memoire" (to remind).

P.P.: Used in written social correspondence, "pour présenter" (to introduce).

P.P.C.: Used in written social correspondence, "pour prendre congé" (to say goodbye).

P.R.: Used in written social correspondence, "pour remercier" (to express thanks).

Persona Non Grata: An individual who is unacceptable to or unwelcome by the host government.

Precedence: Priority; the right to superior honor on a ceremonial or formal occasion; for ambassadors in a country, precedence is determined by the order in which they presented their credentials to the host government.

Protocol : Another name for an agreement. Originally a protocol was considered a somewhat less formal document than a treaty, but that is a distinction no longer valid. A protocol may be an agreement in its own right. It also may constitute added sections which clarify or alter an agreement, or it may be used to add new subjects of agreement to the original document.

Rapporteur: The official of a committee or subcommittee whose job is to prepare a summary report of its discussions and conclusions.

Rapprochment: The establishment of improved relations.

Ratification: The act, subsequent to a treaty's having been negotiated, by which a government commits itself to adhere to that treaty. In the United States, it is inaccurate to speak of the Senate's ratifying a treaty. The executive does this, but only after the Senate has given its consent.

Recognition: Commonly used in connection with the recognition by one state of 1) the existence of another state (for example when a new one is formed), or 2) the existence of a government which is in effective control of a state. The term "de facto recognition" means recognition that a state, or a government of a state, in fact exists – but it also means the withholding of full official recognition of this. When the latter is extended, it is termed "de jure recognition". It is a distinction based more on diplomatic convenience than on logic.

SAARC: South Asian Association for Regional Cooperation, with member states—Afghanistan, Pakistan, Nepal, India, Bangladesh, Bhutan, Sri Lanka and Maldives, is headquartered at Kathmandu (Nepal).

Seventh Floor: Shorthand for the most senior leadership of the U.S. State Department. It is where the offices of the Secretary of State and his most senior aides are located.

Short-Timer: A diplomat whose assignment at a foreign post is nearing its close. A phrase borrowed from the military.

Sixth Floor: Where many of the U.S. State Department's regional and other assistant secretaries have their offices. Shorthand for the assistant secretary level of the department's leadership.

T.D.Y.: Shorthand for a temporary duty assignment.

Tour D'Horizon: A diplomatic discussion covering most (or at least a number of) subjects of current and common concern.

Treaty: A formal mutually binding agreement between countries. The term comes from traiter, to negotiate

Ultimatum: A last statement indicating a final position. On occasion a prelude to the initiation of military action.

Unfriendly Act: A term used when one government wishes to tell another that an action the latter has taken is regarded as so serious that it might lead to a military action against it. An action which risks war.

Vice Consul: A junior ranking consular officer.

Visa: Written authority to enter a country for either temporary or permanent residence, depending on its wording.

Bibliography

Abadi, Jacob. *Israel's Quest for Recognition and Acceptance in Asia: Garrison State Diplomacy*, 2004.

Annual Report, The Ceylon National Chamber of Industries, 1985.

Annual Reports, Indian Council for Cultural Relations, 1978, 1987- 2004, New Delhi.

Annual Reports, Ministry of Commerce and Trade, Government of India, New Delhi 1998-1999, 2001-2004.

Annual Reports, Ministry of External Affairs, Government of India, New Delhi, 1998 - 2005.

Bajpai, Prakash, *Modern Government and Politics* (6 vols.) Anmol, New Dehi, 1994.

Bangladesh police contingent to join UN peacekeeping in Kosovo - People's Daily Online.

Barry Buzan, *Regions and Powers,* 2003.

Bharadwaj, A.N., *Failure of UNO,* Anmol, New Delhi, 1996

Breffni O'Rourke. "South Asia: Afghanistan Joins World's Largest Regional Grouping." Radio Free Europe/ Radio Liberty, 3 April 2007.

Commercial and Economic Reports, High Commission of India Colombo, Dec. 1990, Jan., Feb., April 1991.

Daniel Deudney *Bounding Power: The Republican Security Theory from the Polis to the Global Village.*

Donald Markwell, *John Maynard Keynes and International Relations: Economic Paths to War and Peace*, 2006.

Hans Köchler, *Aussenpolitik und Demokratie* (German), 1986 (Foreign Policy and Democracy).

Hugo Grotius, *The Laws of War and Peace.*

Investment Policy Statement, Government of Sri Lanka, 1990.

Jawaharlal Nehru's Speeches, March 1953-August 1957, 3rd ed. 1963, Publication Division, Ministry of Information and Broadcasting, Government of India, New Delhi.

Jayewardene, J.R., *Man and Memories, Autobiographical Recollection and Reflections,* Vikas Publishing House Pvt. Ltd., 1992.

Katelawala, John, *An Asian Prime Minister Story,* George G. Harrap & Co. Ltd., Britain, 1956.

Lal, Vinod K. et al., *Encyclopaedia of International Laws* (8 vols.), Anmol, New Delhi, 2002.

Malhotra, VK, *Theories and Approaches to International Relations,* Anmol, New Delhi, 1998.

Ministry of Foreign Affairs (Bahrain) (29 May 2008). "Foreign Minister Receives a copy of Credentials of New Four Ambassadors". Press release.

Rahman, Waliur. "US and S Korea to observe SAARC." BBC News, 11 April 2006.

Report National Export Development Plan - 1990 – 94, Sri Lanka Export Development Board, 1991.

Report of Indo-Sri Lanka Joint Commission, Senior Official Meeting 1991, New Delhi.

Report, Indo-Sri Lanka Chamber of Commerce and Industry Colombo, 1985.

Reports Central Bank of Sri Lanka, 1990, Nov. 1993.

Reports of the Second Meeting of India Sri Lanka Joint Business Council March 1992, New Delhi.

Robert H. Jackson *The Global Covenant* 2002.

S.W.R.D. Bandaranaike- Speeches and Writings, Colombo 1963, Department of Information, Government of Ceylon.

S.W.R.D. Bandaranaike The Foreign Policy of Ceylon – Extract from Statements, Colombo, 1954, Department of Information Government of Ceylon.

Security concerns delay India-Bangladesh train link, Reuters, Jul 30, 2007.

Selected Speeches and Writings of Indira Gandhi, Jan-1980-Dec. 1981, Publication Division, Ministry of Information and Broadcasting, Government of India, New Delhi, 1985.

Singh, N.K., *Bangladesh: Diplomacy and Foreign Policy,* Anmol, New Delhi, 2003

Sri Lanka Newest Growth Center in Asia: International Economic Cooperation Division, Ministry of Finance and Planning, Government of Sri Lanka, Colombo.

Statistical Pocket Book of the Democratic Socialist Republic of Sri Lanka, Department of Census and Statistics, Colombo, 1981.

Thondaman, S., *My Life and Time, An Autobiography,* Vol -1, The Media Council, The Cylone Workers Congress, Colombo, 1987.

Index

N

O

P